Running All the
Red Lights

Running All the Red Lights

A Journey of Systemwide Educational Reform

Terry Holliday and Brenda Clark

ASQ Quality Press
Milwaukee, Wisconsin

American Society for Quality, Quality Press, Milwaukee 53203
© 2010 by ASQ
All rights reserved. Published 2009
Printed in the United States of America
15 14 13 12 11 10 09   5 4 3 2 1

Library of Congress Cataloging-in-Publication Data

Holliday, Terry, 1950–
    Running all the red lights / Terry Holliday and Brenda Clark.
       p. cm.
    Includes bibliographical references and index.
    ISBN 978-0-87389-778-5 (soft cover : alk. paper)
    1. School superintendents. 2. School improvement programs. 3. School management
and organization. I. Clark, Brenda, 1947– II. Title.

    LB2831.7.H65 2010
    371.2'07—dc22   2009038271

ISBN: 978-0-87389-778-5

Publisher: William A. Tony
Acquisitions Editor: Matt T. Meinholz
Project Editor: Paul O'Mara
Production Administrator: Randall Benson

ASQ Mission: The American Society for Quality advances individual, organizational,
and community excellence worldwide through learning, quality improvement, and
knowledge exchange.

Attention Bookstores, Wholesalers, Schools, and Corporations: ASQ Quality Press
books, videotapes, audiotapes, and software are available at quantity discounts with
bulk purchases for business, educational, or instructional use. For information,
please contact ASQ Quality Press at 800-248-1946, or write to ASQ Quality Press,
P.O. Box 3005, Milwaukee, WI 53201-3005.

To place orders or to request a free copy of the ASQ Quality Press Publications
Catalog, including ASQ membership information, call 800-248-1946. Visit our
Web site at www.asq.org or http://www.asq.org/quality-press.

Printed in the United States of America

 Printed on acid-free paper

Quality Press
600 N. Plankinton Avenue
Milwaukee, Wisconsin 53203
Call toll free 800-248-1946
Fax 414-272-1734
www.asq.org
http://www.asq.org/quality-press
http://standardsgroup.asq.org
E-mail: authors@asq.org

*To Denise, who has been my solid rock and
inspiration through many turbulent times.*

—Terry Holliday

*In memory of my mother, Anne Tucker Smith, who taught me how
to be a good person by modeling and setting high expectations.
Her example has guided my work and my life. Also to Carol
McCrory for her editing and insights into the flow of the
book, and her unwavering support of the dream.*

—Brenda Clark

Table of Contents

List of Figures and Tables

Acknowledgments

I would like to acknowledge Susan Allred whose consistency in support of children and teachers has always been an inspiration to me. To Dave and Nancy Bayless who have worked diligently to implement data-driven decision making in many school systems across this nation. To Jim Lunsford whose conversations have always been uplifting and inspirational. To the staff of Transylvania and Iredell–Statesville school systems who worked through many versions of classroom improvement strategies to help more children reach success. To Jim and Marie Shipley for their encouragement and support of performance excellence. To Jack Grayson and the staff at American Productivity Quality Council for their vision and leadership in process management. To Brenda Clark who helped me finalize the goal of writing this book and has served as my coach and support through many difficult periods. Finally, to my mom and dad who taught me the work ethic that has served me well through college and 37 years in public education.

—Terry Holliday

I join Terry in extending my thanks and appreciation to Jim and Marie Shipley for providing the support, coaching, encouragement, and opportunity for me to grow in my knowledge and understanding of continual improvement and performance excellence. To Laurel Moore and my many friends in New Mexico who blazed the trail of continuous improvement in classrooms, schools, districts, and state departments against all odds. To Jack Grayson and the staff at American Productivity Quality Council who moved us into the world of process management and enhanced our work. To the staff at Azalea Elementary School (1992–2000) in St. Petersburg, Florida, who taught me that everything we do has to be about the kids and we have to stay focused on that. To my daughter Christi, who gave me insights into the critical issues related to our public education system through the lens of a parent. To the Learning Division team of Iredell–Statesville Schools who turned theory into application, and to all of the many staff members across the district who then worked hard to apply our insights. To Teresa Shade who is my good friend and provides the sanity that I need each day at work. Finally, to Terry and Denise Holliday for the opportunity to join them in Statesville and become part of the work. What a ride it has been!

—Brenda Clark

Introduction

by Terry Holliday

As a school superintendent, I spend a lot of time in communication activities. My general rule of thumb is to spend twice as much time listening as I do talking. My grandmother told me that was why we had two ears and one mouth. My communication tools include blogs, wikis, voice over PowerPoint, speeches, advisory groups, focus groups, newspaper and magazine articles, and Web pages. I have always enjoyed writing and have been trying to write a book for at least the last seven years. I have had numerous partners with whom books were started and publishers contacted; however, the time and topics never seemed to be quite right. I love to read books about educational reform and enjoy listening to books on that remarkable tool, the iPod. And so, with the numerous starts and stops on a book, why now? Why did we finish this one?

IT STARTED AT A RED LIGHT

My friend Carol McCrory suggested the title for the book—*Running All the Red Lights*. She had heard the song "Red Light" by Jonny Lang and thought the song had great lyrics that could serve as a framework for our story. In an odd way, it was the perfect metaphor for our journey of systemwide educational reform in Iredell–Statesville Schools (I–SS).

I was sitting at a red light in Statesville, North Carolina. I had been visiting one of our three central office sites to personally congratulate the staff on our recognition as the 2008 Baldrige award recipient in education. The thing about having to sit at a red light is that you're often forced to just sit and think. It can be a real time to reflect, and that is what happened to me. I thought back on sitting at the same red light some six years earlier. At that time, I had left the superintendency of a comfortable and high-performing school system to take the leadership of a school system in financial and academic trouble—a school system with very low employee morale and even worse community confidence in the system. Six years ago, I was really questioning my decision. The job was looking to be even more difficult than I had expected. Now, sitting at the same red light six years later, this book began to unfold. What are the red lights in education reform? What are the strategies a driver/leader can use in dealing with red lights? When do you stop at a red light, and when do you speed up? When do you turn, and when do you just drive on through?

The red lights in education reform are called different names by different authors. Doug Reeves talks about the *toxic two percent*. John Kotter talks about the *NoNo birds*. Jim Shipley refers to them as the *submarine commanders*. I have also heard them referred to as the gatekeepers for the dogmas of the past. They are the protectors of the status quo.

In my experience, the most significant red lights and the ones that take a lot of time to get through are the citizens themselves. Why? Everyone is an expert in public education. Why? They all went to some kind of school. No matter what strategy leadership wants to use, there are those red lights that want to stop the strategy. Try and lengthen the school day or school year in a school system. The red lights come out very quickly. They say, "no need to lengthen the school day or year, it was good enough for me when I went to school." Try and add technology to schools or create twenty-first century school facilities. The red lights surface overnight—"When I went to school we didn't have all these extras and I turned out just fine."

Another major red light comes from national and state legislative requirements. Requirements such as No Child Left Behind start out as good signals that have the right purpose—to make certain we help all children become successful. However, the signals quickly turn into major red lights that inhibit the success of children. The details of legislation like No Child Left Behind, IDEA, state mandates for financial literacy education, and numerous unfunded mandates quickly become red lights that tie up the progress of our journey to help children reach success.

The red lights that require school superintendents and school principals to spend the most time idling are staff members themselves. Try and implement professional learning communities that require collective inquiry. You will hear things like "leave me alone and let me teach, I don't have time to do my work with all these meetings," "meeting with other teachers is a waste of my time," "when am I going to plan if I spend all my time in meetings with other teachers." The red light that causes a great deal of pain is the red light of low expectations. Working to reach success for all children, the red lights will say things like "these children can't do this," "these kids can't perform at this level because they have no parental support," "these kids can't perform at this level because they are poor and come from a culture of low expectations," "we can't help these kids because the middle school sent them to us unprepared." The red lights that teachers use with children are many. The red lights of ineffective grading practices, teaching focus rather than learning focus, ineffective instructional techniques, and lack of relationships with students are all red lights that stop children on their journey to success.

I meet with parents very often who are red lights to their own children's success. They enable their children to be defiant and to blame others for their lack of success. The parents most often had poor school experiences themselves and they care more about confrontation with school officials to redeem themselves in front of their children than they care about their own child's success.

What can you do as a superintendent, school leader, or classroom leader when you encounter a red light?

You can run a red light. In this book we will give examples of when we ran the red light. Running red lights is appropriate for fire, police, and emergency officials when there is a sense of urgency. There is a great sense of urgency in our school systems to eliminate those negative experiences of children that douse their flame for learning. The dropout crisis in schools across this nation is directly related to the fact that 85 percent of prison inmates are high school dropouts. The current economic crisis in our country can only be addressed through a sense of urgency with education.

You can reflect at a red light. In this book we will talk about tools and techniques for reflection when you are confronted with a red light. In our school improvement plan framework and our basic tool of the plan–do–study–act cycle, school leaders and teachers will find tools of reflection.

You can turn right at a red light, with caution. How do you know when to change direction when you encounter a red light? How do you know that the detour you take when turning right will eventually get you to your destination? Through our discussion about mission, vision, values, and alignment, we will give you insight on how to turn right at the red light and still be able to reach your destination of success for children.

You can back up at a red light. What happens when you are going too fast and you get caught in the intersection at a red light? You have to back up with caution not to hit anyone behind you. In this book we will describe those times when we were going too fast and got caught in the intersection and had to back up. We will provide tools of communication, planning, collaboration, and deployment that can help you back up without hitting anyone behind you or being hit by traffic coming through the intersection.

When faced with a long stretch of red lights on a busy road, there are three strategies that drivers or leaders can utilize to arrive at their destination.

You can use the rabbit start-and-stop strategy. We have all seen these leaders. They race off as quickly as the red light changes only to have to stop at the next red light. School superintendents and principals often use this strategy upon returning from the most recent conference or inspirational speech. They burn rubber out of the red light with new vigor and enthusiasm, only to come to a squealing stop at the next red light. This approach wastes a lot of energy and is very costly for "brake systems" and "tires."

You can change lanes between red lights. These leaders are always changing lanes and trying to find the lane that will get them through the red lights as fast as possible. These leaders are much like the rabbit strategy leaders. They may start fast out of a red light and then switch lanes whenever they see an opening in hopes of getting through the red lights before they change. These leaders cause many wrecks in an organization. Those in the organization who are moving along with one strategy are often blindsided when the leader changes direction and the other drivers have to slam on their brakes. The ripple effect usually leads to wrecks that slow down the entire traffic flow on the highway within the organization while the leader is still changing lanes miles ahead, never looking back to see what damage he might have caused. These are the superintendents who come in as change agents and make a number of lane changes and then are quickly off to other locations to speed up their school system's change efforts. This strategy might work in the very short term; however, it will cause many wrecks and much damage in the long run.

The final strategy is the one that requires the driver to look forward *and* backward. It is the *strategy of persistence.* This is the strategy of maintaining a steady speed since the red lights are probably based on a timer. The leader who keeps a steady speed and is always looking forward and backward to change lanes, cautiously, with plenty of planning and preparation, can usually get through the maze of red lights and reach the destination quicker than with most of the other strategies. Following this approach will certainly result in fewer opportunities for wrecks and damage to other cars and other drivers.

So, while sitting at a red light and reflecting on the journey we have taken in I–SS, we have at times seen all the red lights and utilized all the strategies to deal with red lights. This book is about that journey. Our journey has been a destination of success for all children. Even if *we* never reach the end of the journey, we must prepare our organization to sustain that journey once we, as leaders, are gone. We also hope to inspire other leaders in other school systems to sustain their journeys toward success for all children. Whatever strategy you choose to use in dealing with red lights, we hope that you will never give up just because you encounter one. The journey is frustrating, but the destination is always worth the trouble of the trip.

1

Red Light #1—Placing Blame on External Sources

by Terry Holliday

November, 2002. I was sitting at a red light in Statesville, North Carolina. It was cold and rainy, and as I looked down the street I began to question why I had come to this superintendent's job at this time. I was really missing the security of my former job where the school system was among the highest-performing in the state, educators were respected, and the community fully supported what we were trying to do. I was in transit to one of my listening sessions with faculty and staff and it had begun to dawn on me that the job was going to be much more difficult than I had imagined. I am getting ahead of myself here, however, but that is what you often do at a red light. You reflect and make a decision to continue to move in the direction in which you were headed or you make a decision to turn right on red. Of course, you can run the red light, but if you do that, you'd better make certain you have the authority and urgency to run the light.

While sitting at the red light I reflected on what I had gotten myself into with the superintendent's job for this school system. During the interview process for the superintendent's job, I had done my homework. I had read the local newspaper, talked with fellow superintendents, called friends who worked in the school system, and analyzed all the data about the school system. What I found was an exciting challenge and opportunity. The superintendent had just been fired for financial mismanagement. The firing was contested, and there was a very public and lengthy trial that documented all of the charges. As a matter of fact, the charges against the superintendent had been publicized on the school system's Web page. The charges were picked up by the local newspaper and by television channels in the area. The school system had made promises to citizens and to staff that included new schools, new programs, and high levels of academic performance. Staff members had been promised large increases in local supplements, new programs, technology, and new facilities. The scandal wiped out public trust in the school system. Not only had the superintendent been accused of financial mismanagement, but the school board had also taken a trip to a national convention and there were numerous allegations of expenditures on improper items. Public confidence in the school system was at an all-time low.

The data I had gathered while preparing for the interview told an interesting story. The school system was a fast-growing district due to its proximity to a major urban area. While the school system was fast growing, the growth was mixed between middle/upper income and the challenging demographics of minority and poverty-based populations. The school system was mired in mediocrity. North Carolina was well known nationally in the 1990s for the development of a statewide accountability system. The accountability system had state-developed standards, state-developed assessments, and a student growth model that was the envy of most states. With a statewide accountability system, however, there were also statewide comparisons between districts. Comparisons were available for math, reading, and writing in grades 3 through 8 and 10 high school subjects. The school system I had been charged to lead was performing well below state averages on all assessments, and in many cases was among the bottom third of school districts in North Carolina. Dropout rates were among the highest in the state, SAT scores were below state and national averages, and school attendance was among the lowest in the state. Additionally, the school district was considered fairly wealthy based on property values, which meant that state funding was low. State funding formulas at that time provided equity funding for school systems with a low property tax value. Also, the school system was in a county that was very conservative and maintained a very low tax rate. A low tax rate translated into low per-pupil funding from local revenues. The school system also ranked among the 10 lowest in the state for per-pupil funding for operating expenses.

As the light turned green, I kept moving in the direction I was headed. Having a direction is a necessity when you are on a trip. My immediate destination was the next school on the listening tour. Why was I doing a listening tour? The real reason was that I needed to indirectly let people know what our direction as a school system was going to be. I also needed to find out where the red lights were on this trip and to figure out what was preventing us from reaching our destination. A listening tour is a tool used by many leaders who are new to a position. Just since we began writing this book, North Carolina has elected a new governor who has been engaged in a listening tour during the 60-day transition from election to taking office. Many elected officials and newly appointed CEOs engage in listening tours in order to find out what is happening, why it is happening, and in what directions they need to lead the organization. My listening tour

> 1. *What is getting in the way of student learning?*
> 2. *What do you need to help all children succeed?*
> 3. *What do you expect from me as superintendent?*

Figure 1.1 Three questions for listening tour.

included visits to 32 school sites and three support sites. I informed staff at each site as to the time of my visit. I provided cookies, punch, and coffee. I posted three large poster sheets and provided sticky notes for all staff to respond to questions. I told staff I would be asking three basic questions, and their responses would give me direction on what needed to be done in the school system within my first year as superintendent (see Figure 1.1). I left the poster sheets at each site for three to five days and then collected all the posters and placed them on the wall in our school board room. I had the superintendent's cabinet assist me in "affinitizing" the responses. I then sent the affinitized list back to each staff and had them rank the priorities for each question. When I had all priorities ranked by site, I compiled the results for the entire district and then had school board members, parents, and staff members rank the top ten issues that needed to be addressed for each question (see Figure 1.2). The overall district priorities for questions 1 and 2 became the direction for my work as superintendent, helped prioritize budget requests, and helped provide direction to the board of education. The responses to question 3 became the basis for my evaluation as superintendent and provided an excellent vehicle for a 360 feedback process.* Six years later, I continue to tell staff that they told me what was important that I do as superintendent. I tell them I do that, then tell them what I have done, and they provide me feedback on how well my actions are impacting their expectations.

#1—*What is getting in the way of student learning?* By asking this question, I was indirectly letting *all* staff know the direction of the school system—increasing student learning. The school system had developed a mission statement during an intensive strategic planning session a few years previously. The mission statement was, "our school system will rigorously challenge all students to achieve their academic potential and to

---

* A 360 process refers to asking stakeholders what is expected of you as the leader, reporting back to stakeholders how you will meet their expectations, and then measuring how well you met their expectations.

What is getting in the way of student learning?
1. Poor student attendance
2. Lack of parental support
3. Inadequate facilities
4. Inadequate supplies, materials, and technology
5. Paperwork and meetings

What do you need to help all children succeed?
1. Smaller class size
2. Funding for materials and equipment
3. Improved facilities
4. Reduced paperwork
5. More technology

What do you expect from me as superintendent?
1. Visibility
2. Support for all programs
3. Improved communication
4. Leadership
5. Honesty

Figure 1.2   Top five responses to questions.

lead productive and rewarding lives. We will achieve this mission with the support of parents, staff, and the community." The mission statement was excellent. The problem was that very few staff members, students, parents, and board members really knew what it said. It was also evident from the data that very few staff members were living the mission statement. It was evident from responses to this question that several concepts from the mission statement were either not understood or completely ignored. *Rigorously challenging* curriculum was something only a few students received, and *all children* reaching their academic potential was not something that was being practiced (as evidenced by the large achievement gaps among student subgroups). It was quite evident from the responses to this question that we had a belief problem. If you do not *believe* you can reach your destination, then no one will take the trip—much less plan for the trip.

Another thing that became quite clear from the responses I received was that staff members were prone to blame the lack of student success on external factors. For example, "apathetic and unmotivated students" was the number one response to the question. Another frequently cited reason was lack of parental support. Other items that bubbled up to top ten status were lack of facilities, lack of funding, class sizes too large, not enough planning time, lack of technology, lack of supplies and material, and lack of community support. Most of us do this, especially when we are traveling. When we get delayed in traffic and hit a lot of red lights that delay us from reaching our appointment at the correct time we blame the traffic, other drivers, the weather, road construction, and the "idiot" who set the timing on the red lights. It is unusual for us to self-reflect and properly place responsibility for our tardiness on the fact that we did not budget sufficient time for our trip. Educators are very quick to list the things that are getting in the way of student learning, and the list usually includes all those things over which we have little control. The reason is human nature. We are hardwired to blame others, and external factors, because it is much easier and requires very little effort on our part to change. I could tell that the job was going to be difficult. Changing beliefs of educators is difficult and in many cases almost impossible (Fullan 2008; Reeves 2008; DuFour, DuFour, and Eaker 2008). I knew I was going to have to start the change process by building relationships and then requiring modest changes in behavior. The highlight of the information was that I now knew the enormity of the challenge.

#2—*What do you need to help all children succeed?* The purpose of this question was to align resources to the mission statement. However, very few staff members understood the reason behind the question, and even fewer believed that something would actually come of the responses. I used the same process with the poster sheets, sticky notes, affinity process, ranking, and communication. It was interesting to note what staff members ranked as one of the highest needs—holding children and parents accountable for student attendance. It was evident that the school system had a student attendance problem based on the attendance percentage and relatively low rank among other state school systems. It was interesting that staff members associated the enforcement of student attendance with more children reaching success. My practical experience over 30 years in education had shown that student engagement while being in attendance is much more important than just being in attendance. However, it was important to honor teacher opinions and begin to focus on improving student attendance.

Other items that made the top ten were follow-ups to responses to question #1. Staff wanted more "stuff." They wanted improved facilities, more technology, more administrative support, more parental support, more school board support, more community support, more supplies and materials, more equipment, more planning time, and lower class size. Again, all the items related to external factors. What could *other* people or entities do to help students become more successful?

What really surprised the entire staff was that the list became the basis for budget priorities during budget preparation for the new school year. I received many comments from staff like "We didn't know you would really use our comments," "Lots of people have asked us what we think; however, no one has ever done anything with our opinions," "If I had known you would really do something, I would have been more thoughtful about my response." The board of education was especially surprised at the new budget process. Several board members were concerned that their pet projects were not high on the budget priority list and several were perturbed that I had positioned them in such a way that listing their pet projects above staff requests could have a negative impact on their next election.

#3—What do you expect from me as superintendent? This was a crucial question. I had recently been trained in a 360 feedback process and I knew that the responses could be the basis for an eventual superintendent evaluation. Also, I knew that trust in the superintendent's position needed to be restored. The responses were no surprise given what the staff had recently endured when the previous superintendent was fired. The staff wanted me to be visible. They wanted me to get in the schools and see what the "real world" was like. They wanted me to attend student events and be supportive of all programs. They also wanted me to communicate openly and honestly.

I took the staff feedback and established several goals as superintendent. I made a commitment to visit every school, every quarter (35 schools). So now I track my visits on the wall on the board conference room so the board and staff members who visit the room can see that I take this goal seriously. For communication, I made a goal to meet with each staff at least twice a year. For the community, I made a goal of writing an article for the local newspaper at least quarterly.

During staff meetings I do things like provide short updates on the progress of the school system, provide updates on external issues that are impacting the school system, and provide time for questions and answers. During the last six years, we have greatly improved our communication capabilities, and now I have a blog, superintendent e-mail, voice over PowerPoint presentations, video updates, RSS feeds, podcasting, archived presentation pages, and a local cable channel that provides time for educational updates. Every year I send out a survey that asks respondents to anonymously rate my visibility, communication, and support of programs (see Figure 1.3). The board of education uses those results during my annual evaluation process.

Question	03–04	04–05	05–06	06–07	07–08
Superintendent has been visible . . .	90%	88%	76%	90%	92%
Superintendent has been supportive . . .	92%	91%	92%	93%	94%
Superintendent has improved communication . . .	93%	81%	84%	87%	88%
Superintendent has clearly established direction . . .	93%	98%	98%	99%	99%
Superintendent decisions and actions are student centered	93%	88%	85%	93%	93%

Figure 1.3   Superintendent 360 survey.

CONNECTING TO RESEARCH

What I had discovered on the listening tour were several red lights that I had not fully anticipated. The first red light is well documented in research. People who are determined not to act can always find a reason to justify inaction, and the reason is usually external to their behavior. Seldom do we look at having to change ourselves in order to get better results. In *On Common Ground* (2005) Barth et al. talk about the barriers to education reform and how to overcome them. Rick DuFour documents a meeting he had with a high school staff where he asked for their ideas for improving student achievement. The list looks very similar to the list that I developed as a summary of my listening tour. The DuFour list includes: more financial support, smaller class sizes, more support staff, fewer preparations, more supportive parents, abolishing state assessments, fewer initiatives from central office, better facilities, and of course more motivated students. The mantra "blame external sources for low student performance" is prevalent in our nation's schools.

Every time I ask an audience of superintendents if they have ever heard their teachers say, "leave me alone, provide me with what I need, and let me teach," almost 100 percent of the audience will raise their hands. Nowhere in my listening tour list nor in the DuFour list do you see things like 1) provide all students with access to a viable and guaranteed curriculum, 2) closely monitor all students' achievement and provide immediate and effective interventions, 3) provide meaningful and timely information to teachers, and 4) provide training and tools to transition from a teaching system to a learning system. While it is important to validate teacher concerns about the need to improve external resources, it is also important to have teachers recognize that the internal resources and those things that schools can control will eventually have more impact on improving student learning than the external issues. Also, we can implement the internal changes that need to be made much more quickly than we can address the external changes.

Another red light that I discovered was that the relationship between central office—and more importantly, the superintendent and board of education—and the school staff was at an all-time low. I immediately realized that top-down initiatives and mandates were not going to work. In spite of a sense of urgency for reform that would raise student achievement, I knew that I had to build relationships before I could mandate change. Alan Deutschman in his book *Change or Die* (2007) is very clear about the importance of relationships. Deutschman asks readers, if they knew they were going to die if they did not change their behaviors, what percentage would actually change their behaviors? He documents research from the medical community concerning heart bypass patients. When faced with the challenge of changing behaviors such as smoking, drinking, and overeating, and when pressed to exercise more and relieve stress, only one out of 10 patients actually make the necessary changes. Deutschman documents that a focus on facts, fear, and force defeats the necessary change in behaviors. Deutschman focuses on the three R's—relate, repeat, and reframe. *Relate* means building relationships. *Repeat* means starting with small behavior changes and then repeating those behavior changes until people actually begin to *"reframe"* their outlook on life and their beliefs.

This red light of relationships did cause me to slightly change direction. While the destination of the trip did not change, the actual directional path did change. A key to the directional change was communication. By going to each site and showing that I valued the responses through my follow-up on the responses, I began to build the relationship through trust and open communication. The staff at each site knew what they had written on the responses. They knew that I had been honest in listing exactly what they had said, and I was beginning to model an expectation of transparency in the school system for data and communication. Staff members had grown accustomed to the public relations spin, and trust in the superintendent and central office was very low. Rebuilding a relationship of trust and open communication was vital prior to requiring behavior changes from staff.

John Kotter in his recent book *A Sense of Urgency* (2008) discusses eight actions for success in a changing world. One key strategy is building a sense of urgency for change. Kotter recommends several steps in implementing this strategy. One of the key steps is to bring the outside in through listening to employees who interface directly with customers, share what is learned through the listening, and publicly display the gathered data. By listening directly to teachers and staff who interacted every day with our customers (students), sharing back with them what was learned, and publicly posting the data gathered, I had begun the development of a sense of urgency. Also, through the listening tour and follow-up, I had modeled many quality tools. I had modeled the use of an issue bin through the three questions and the responses on sticky notes. I had modeled the use of an affinity process. I had modeled the use of light voting to rank and prioritize items on a list. I had modeled open communication and visibility by my visits to schools. I had brought the outside in by modeling rather than mandating the use of quality tools. Perhaps the best modeling was the plan–do–study–act process for the number one response to question #2—"Do something about student attendance!!!!"

A FOCUS ON RESULTS

Deutschman talks about relationships being a key to implementing change. The next step is to change behaviors before you expect people to change beliefs. Slight changes in behavior that show short-term success are crucial to changing an organization like a school system. The staff had listed student attendance as the top priority for change in order to help more students be successful. I tackled this issue through the modeling of a plan–do–study–act cycle. I did not take a lot of time in training the team that I assembled to work on this problem. I modeled the steps in a PDSA cycle (see Figure 1.4) and began the process of action research.

1. Validate the need for improvement
2. Clarify purpose, goals, and measures
3. Adopt and deploy an approach to continual improvement
4. Translate the approach to aligned action
5. Analyze results
6. Make improvements

Figure 1.4 Six steps of the plan–do–study–act cycle.
© Jim Shipley & Associates, Inc.

The first step was to validate the need for improvement. The team had no idea that our student attendance was among the lowest in the state. The board of education was even more surprised. When we analyzed the data, we found that the lowest-performing schools were secondary schools and schools with large populations of lower socioeconomic status students. We also gathered data through parent, student, and staff meetings as to possible reasons for the low attendance percentage. Staff members identified the lack of a clear policy on attendance and lack of enforcement of existing state regulations concerning student attendance as key reasons for our results. The feedback and data analysis provided the team with the goal for student attendance. We would improve student attendance so that our school system would become a top-ten performer among school systems in the state.

The next step was to create a strategy for achieving that goal. The strategy was to revise the school district policy for student attendance. The revision of the policy was based on best-practice school systems in our state. We looked at the top ten school systems for student attendance and asked for a copy of their policies. The team analyzed the policies and rewrote our school system policy to reflect those best-practice school systems. Then the *big step.* We actually had to do something with the policy. In other words, there had to be deployment of the strategy. The data system had to be upgraded and student attendance makeup procedures had to be developed. Communication to students, parents, and staff was crucial to the deployment. Also, every school had to develop a specific goal in the school improvement plan with specific deployment steps that identified persons responsible and resources needed and tracked attendance percentages monthly. With the deployment, we now had a method of tracking our student attendance every month and making adjustments to the deployment plan. Through our monthly team meetings we began to identify those schools that were improving student attendance and those schools that were not improving. Principal meetings began to focus on sharing best practices for improving student attendance, and principal coaching and evaluation sessions always had some focus on student attendance. When we looked at the results at the end of the year, we were amazed. We had improved from 75th among the 115 North Carolina school systems to 55th (see Figure 1.5).

Figure 1.5 shows I–SS performance on student attendance since the inception of the first PDSA initiative. Our school system consistently ranks in the top five, and the average of the last three years' performance shows that our school system ranks third in the state for student attendance.

To staff members, student attendance was a huge red light that was consistently stopping them from reaching the destination of student success. By modeling a process of reflection at the red light and then mapping

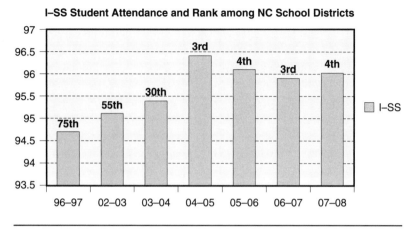

Figure 1.5   I–SS student attendance results using PDSA.

an improvement cycle that would allow us to go through more green lights, we had begun the change process from always blaming external factors to making a change in internal behaviors that could lead to improved student performance.

The eventual result of the listening tour was the development of a district vision statement that served as the rallying cry for our entire school system. By the end of the year and with our success on student attendance, the board of education adopted a vision statement asserting that our school system would become a top-ten performing school system in North Carolina. The destination was now official. We set timelines. We established a strategic plan with specific goals that would drive us toward interim steps in reaching the vision. We established clear interim goals that would push us to above state averages in three years, above region and comparison district averages in five years, and top ten in our state within seven years. This journey was not going to be a rabbit start-and-stop journey like some drivers/ leaders do when trying to race to a destination. This journey was about a steady pace that would allow us to go through green lights rather than be stopped at red lights. It was now time to bring in the outside. I had worked closely with Jim Shipley & Associates while in a previous school system. One of their consultants (Brenda Clark) had proven to be very effective in getting schools to understand the work that needed to be done once a school district has identified the goals of a strategic plan. After all, no matter how great your district strategic plan is, it is only a collection of words. Our schools and school leaders needed training in how to turn the strategic plan *words* into school improvement *plans* with clear school-level goals and clear action steps. I invited Brenda to do a workshop for school and district leaders here in Statesville. We wanted the setting to be very positive since this was the first "official" continuous improvement training. We set Brenda up for training in a wonderful state park setting and made certain to provide her with the tools and materials she needed to have a successful training.

2

Red Light #2—
Complacency

by Brenda Clark

Upon retiring from Pinellas County, Florida, after serving as principal of Azalea Elementary—winner of the Governor's Sterling Award for Performance Excellence—I became what Terry Holliday affectionately calls a "highly paid consultant." It was in this part of my career that I found myself in a high-performing district in western North Carolina, in a small room with a collection of resistant learners who were "chosen" by the superintendent to participate in a new approach to improving student achievement called *systems improvement*. Kotter, in his book *A Sense of Urgency* (2008), speaks of the serious problem we have with complacency, and I was facing complacency in this room of educators who wondered why they had to learn about systems improvement when they were already high performing.

As the morning moved forward, a man appeared in the door, sat for a few minutes to listen, and then left. When I asked who he was I was told that he was the superintendent, Dr. Terry Holliday. That was my introduction to a person who would invite me to join him in his journey toward performance excellence, first as a "highly paid consultant" and later as a coach, mentor, ruthlessly compassionate friend, and coworker. While I didn't realize it that morning, I had just met the person with whom I would become a co-learner as we tried to figure out how to apply systems work to the world of education.

I worked with Terry in that district and, when he moved to Iredell–Statesville, he called me to come and work with him there. He had completed all of his listening sessions in I–SS, defined the priorities for the work, and set attendance as the focus of a districtwide PDSA. As the "highly paid consultant" it became my job to help people at the school level understand how to use a systems approach to create processes that would improve attendance. As he did in the previous district, Terry arranged for me to be in a room too small for the number of people attending, and as before, they had no idea why they had to be part of this new systems thing. Kotter has it right . . . complacency is the first barrier that has to be broken.

My first workshop to impart wisdom about systems and PDSA was at Lake Norman State Park. While this sounds like an ideal place to go for a learning experience, the five-mile trip into the park obeying the 25 mile per hour speed limit being enforced by a rabid park ranger did not put the participants in a learning mood. Add to that Kotter's complacency insights, compounded by the feeling that this was just another thing that would go away when this superintendent departs, and you have the perfect storm for a disaster in learning. School teams came for two days of group learning, which meant I was there for four days with school teams, and they added one day with the district office employees so they could get an idea of this systems stuff as well. Can you see the perfect storm brewing?

It is easy for me to reflect on this and see what went wrong. I was doing what I was hired to do—teach these folks about systems work for two eight-hour sessions so they could go out and practice PDSA on attendance. What I didn't know then and have learned since is that adult learners are just like kids, they don't come highly motivated just because they have grown up. Rather to the contrary, they have become less motivated and are more skeptical of the learning as they have been involved in so much "teaching" that has resulted in so little applicable "learning" in their lives that they don't want two more days of "teaching" about stuff, in their opinion, they don't need.

I was at a red light and didn't realize it. For decades we have provided professional development for educators based on the flavor of the month, and mostly the delivery model is "sit and get." As a "highly paid consultant" that was what I did because I could only be there for a few days and I needed to teach them everything I knew so they could do the work when I was gone. The "teach" versus "learn" approach was driven by the schedule rather than by what was needed. In a learning model, the delivery of content is matched equally, with the same amount of time spent on modeling, practice, feedback, and coaching over time. The learning environment becomes one of practice and application to improve the day-to-day work.

When the light turned green I started teaching, and by the end of the week we had accomplished the following:

- About 10 percent of the participants were intrigued by the information and wanted to try the systems approach.

- The other 90 percent were at various stages of acceptance of the new approach from wanting to know more to out-and-out resentment and denial.

- Two tickets were given out by the park ranger after he came into the workshop and lectured all of us on the speed limit.

- After five days straight of the same lunch I never wanted to see potato salad again, even though I was raised in the South!

CONNECTING TO RESEARCH

Michael Fullan in his book *The Six Secrets of Change* (2008) refers to the third secret as being "capacity building." Building the capacity of your workforce to do the work that needs to be done requires a carefully designed approach to professional development that aligns the plan to the needs of the workers, not the needs of the professional development calendar or the schedule of the highly paid consultant. Fullan points out that "capacity building entails leaders investing in the development of individual and collaborative efficacy of a whole group or system to accomplish significant improvements." If we are going to ask people to act differently, then we must develop their capacity to do so.

As we said in Chapter 1, seldom do we look at having to change ourselves in order to get better results, and one of the most difficult parts of the three R's in changing our behavior is *repeat*. Starting with small behavior changes that we will repeat means we must know what that behavior change looks like and how we should do it. Professional development is essential to knowing how to change our behavior in a positive manner. The National Staff Development Council recommends that for every hour of content delivered in professional development, you provide seven hours of modeling, practice, feedback, and coaching. This approach ensures that participants are provided the content, given a visual of what application looks like, have the opportunity to practice, and are given feedback and coaching based on that practice so they get better at application. This approach will change behavior because it engages participants in reframing their outlook and their beliefs. The results of providing a model that ensures that participants will act their way into a new way of thinking are documented in Table 2.1.

Think back to the crowded room at Lake Norman State Park with the reluctant participants and the two-day consultant. The two days of training did not result in broad application across the district because the purpose of the event was to deliver information, or content. Without relevant modeling and participant practice that results in feedback and coaching, knowledge of content does not move beyond whatever is remembered by each participant

Table 2.1   Effectiveness of professional development activities.

Presentation model	Knowledge	Skill acquisition	Classroom application	Student effect sizes
Present information	40–80%	10%	5%	0.01
Present + model	80–85%	10–40%	5–10%	0.03
Present + model + practice + feedback	80–85%	80%	10–15%	0.39
Present + model + practice + feedback + coaching	90%	90%	80–90%	1.68

Source: www.nrcld.org/about/presentations/2004/IDA_Chicago_Dec2004.ppt.

and what they choose to do with that new knowledge once they are back in the complex world of their day-to-day work.

A FOCUS ON RESULTS

While student attendance was identified as the red light for the district, and PDSA was the approach that was to be used, capacity of the staff to apply a PDSA approach to improving attendance was limited. Professional development for the workers at the school level had to be provided so they would have the capacity to implement an action research–based approach to improving attendance based on the gaps at their individual schools. Fullan's (2008) fourth secret to change is "learning is the work." He emphasizes the need for learning while doing and not getting caught up in the workshop mentality of learning for workers when training.

The two days of learning for the school teams was focused on developing their skills in utilizing a PDSA approach to improving attendance for their site based on their data. It was also a theory-based systems learning experience to support the district's foundational approach to systems improvement.

The result of this experience for both school teams and the central office participants was application practice with PDSA on a district gap that needed to be closed—attendance. Practicing with a real issue is essential to learning, and leadership selected an issue that was defined by the employees rather than using a top-down approach. This created buy-in to the work and set up the application experience as an easy win. It is important that learners experience success in the application; thus, selecting a less complex issue that will ensure some amount of success is necessary to build confidence and buy-in.

The theory-based systems training, which was also part of the two days, laid the foundation for the next wave of training, which would focus on school improvement planning. The district journey toward continual improvement had been expanded to the school leadership level, and connections between the district level and the schools were established through a common issue. Bringing the outside in was continued in this professional development experience.

For me, as a "highly paid consultant," it was five days in a district with educators struggling with issues similar to those educators across the United States struggle with, and similar to my own struggles as an educator for 30 years. The red light was building the capacity of the workers to think differently and do different work. With new knowledge came a green light, and we moved forward in beginning to understand the *application* of PDSA in the work. On the horizon I could clearly see the next red light shining. The next red light was strategic planning and connecting it to PDSA, which was foreign thinking in the assembly-line approach to educating children. As Terry indicated in Chapter 1, we were off to a start, but not burning rubber and not starting and stopping. The journey would be one of consistent movement forward and on to the challenge of understanding strategic planning at the school level.

3

Red Light #3—Cultural Barriers

by Brenda Clark

The "week in the park" consulting event resulted in middle management (principals, assistant principals, district department leads) across the district being exposed to the direction and vision of the new superintendent. He had been modeling continuous improvement with small groups at all levels of the organization since taking over, but this was the first formal presentation of the approach presented to a designated leadership group. While received positively by about 10 percent of the participants, the majority of school and district folks were somewhere between curious, to openly skeptical, to downright opposed to continual improvement and systems work. Applying this work to a real-life issue such as student attendance grounded the new approach in a gap that needed to be closed and added a data-supported sense of urgency to the work. The "week in the park," however, was no "walk in the park."

My next trip to I–SS was focused on the concepts and skills behind strategic planning. I was given the challenge of tying the previous work on plan–do–study–act cycles for improving attendance to the superintendent's requirement that every school create a strategic goal based on its gap in attendance and then implement a deployment plan to close that gap through its school improvement plan (SIP). This was the beginning of the tough work of cultural change. I was facing a yellow light that was turning red. We were moving further into significant cultural change for the district folks, and the caution light was tinged pink and rapidly becoming red based on the looks on the participants' faces.

Strategic planning in education has long been considered an oxymoron since we as educators have mostly depended on the textbook people to tell us what to teach and how to teach it. We have never given much thought to using data to determine student performance on the essential knowledge that students must master. As a principal, I often met great resistance from teachers when I asked for daily lesson plans, and I was about to ask principals and district department leaders to create and implement a strategic plan. It crossed my mind that perhaps I had moved into "not so highly paid" status based on the work I would need to do to change the cultural beliefs surrounding planning in education.

Educational organizations have been doing business as usual for centuries and, as we discussed in Chapter 1, everyone knows what schools look like—especially those people charged with running them. Strategic planning is relatively new to the educational environment. Within the last 20 to 30 years, strategic plans have become a requirement for schools and districts. Prior to that time, school and district direction was driven by content within textbooks. The objective was to finish the textbook in one year, and the "teaching" approach was used to do this. Learning, if measured at all, was only measured by the grade book and report card. Data across districts, schools, classrooms, and departments were not collected, analyzed, shared, or utilized in making decisions about what to do next. Strategic planning was not an approach used in education.

Our district had made progress on increasing student attendance through the districtwide PDSA on attendance, the improved board of education student attendance policy, and the data system that provided monthly updates and comparison data from school to school. Without a strategic plan, the superintendent knew that the district had made about as much progress as possible. Moving an organization from a textbook-driven culture to a strategic goal–driven culture based on data-driven decision making was a daunting undertaking, but the foundational PDSA and systems work was the springboard needed to move forward.

My work as a consultant had given me the opportunity to work at the state level in New Mexico where I was part of designing the school improvement planning approach for the entire state. We reviewed the work of six states and it became evident that there were foundational parts to a strategic plan that were key to successful implementation. Long-range goals, clarified by short-term target goals, supported by clearly defined strategies to achieve those goals are nonnegotiable requirements. Let me repeat that: long-range goals, clarified by short-term target goals, supported by clearly defined strategies to achieve those goals are nonnegotiable requirements. As I reflect on that now, it seems so simple, but, at that time, I quickly learned that goal writing did not come naturally to many educators and certainly not those at the school level. So, we had work to do.

At I–SS, our first task was to teach leadership teams how to write SMART *(specific, measurable, aligned, results oriented, time bound)* goals based on urgent gaps identified through data. We focused on attendance, utilized the individual data from each school, and developed a three-year, long-term goal clarified by a one-year target goal and supported by an identified strategy for improvement. Once school leadership teams were successfully able to develop these three components in the area of attendance, we worked on creating the step-by-step deployment plan for the strategy. Several coaching sessions were required over a period of three years before school leadership teams, led by principals, were able to successfully create an action-driven school improvement plan (SIP) based on gaps determined through data, relative to key areas of improvement.

The use of a template for school improvement planning was key to the consistency that was needed to create strategic plans that would do more than sit on a shelf. When we started the process, the SIP was a one-year plan and proved to be overwhelming to school leadership teams, so we shortened it. We improved the template by marrying the concept of PDSA with the strategic planning template and created a planning process that was implemented quarter by quarter with data driving the improvements needed in the deployment plans at the end of each quarter. The transition to quarterly planning deployment plans gave clarity to the process and provided leadership teams the opportunity to engage their staff in the work that needed to be completed for that quarter.

The template requires a three-year goal, followed by a target goal, and includes the data that led to the selection of the goal (see Figure 3.1). It also requires that the approach for the quarter be identified and that deployment, fidelity of implementation, and impact measures be determined within the action plan for the approach. The action plan is the work the goal teams will do to implement the approach and work toward achievement of the goal. Data from the measures are collected at the end of the quarter, and a consistent data analysis process using four key questions is applied within the template to provide information and direction for the next quarter's deployment plan.

Creating a consistent approach to strategic planning enabled us to train, coach, and support school leadership teams across the district to become high-performing teams in terms of strategic planning and deployment. The innovation in the process occurs in the selection of the approach and deployment plan. All of the schools in the district have the same goal of closing the reading gap, but selecting the right approach to reach that goal is where innovation and creative use of resources come into play. As Fullan (2008) describes it, there is an Accenture ad with Tiger Woods that says, "relentless consistency, 50 percent; willingness to change, 50 percent." Just like in this ad, consistency in key processes causes people to practice behaviors that become the culture of the organization. The school improvement planning approach is part of the culture of the district, and data drives the

School name:	Year:	Current NCLB status:	Current ABC status:

P	Plan: Identify the gap and the approach.

Overall SMART Goal (Three-year projection):

Insert (or attach) data table to support the selection of the above stated overall SMART Goal:

Data Analysis. Answer the data analysis questions.

1. What are the key strengths and data to support them?	2. What are the key opportunities for improvement and the data to support them?	3. What information/data are needed that we do not have?

Target SMART Goal (One-year projection based on the gap analysis in question 2 above):

4. What is your next step? (Identify key approach or strategy you will implement during cycle 1 to achieve your target goal)

D	Do: Develop and implement deployment plan.

Step #	Cycle 1 detailed steps	Person(s) responsible	Measure/ indicator	Start date	End date
#1					

Deployment Plan Quality Check:

What resources/budget needs do you have for the first cycle?

Figure 3.1 School improvement planning template. *Continued*

If you identified budget needs, what budget code will you use to meet the budget needs for this cycle? If funding is not available, identify the steps from the deployment plan that will address the funding gap.	

What professional development, if any, will be offered in cycle 1 to support the staff in implementing the approach?

Determine the measures/data that will be used to determine the effectiveness of the first-cycle approach by answering the following questions:		
A. What data will you use to determine if the approach was deployed?	B. What data will you use to determine if the approach was deployed with fidelity?	C. What data will you use to determine if the approach impacted the overall goal or target goal?

S	**Study: Analysis of data after implementing approach.**

At the end of cycle 1, answer the following questions based on the data collected from your identified measures:		
1. What are the key strengths and data to support them?	2. What are the key opportunities for improvement and the data to support them?	3. What information/data are needed that we do not have?

Reflect on the data analysis for cycle 1. Which option best describes your direction for cycle 2 (double-click the box and select "check" to check the box)?	
☐ Target goal has been met and is changed to reflect new target. ☐ Target goal not met, but data indicates current approach is effective so we will continue current approach and repeat deployment plan for the next cycle.	☐ Target goal not met so we will continue current approach but make improvements to deployment plan based on data analysis above. ☐ Target goal not met, and data indicates gap is widening so we will abandon current approach and identify a new approach.

A	**Act: Revise or continue with deployment plan based on data analysis.**

4. What is your next step for cycle 2? Identify key approach or strategy. (If you are continuing with the approach from cycle 1, restate it here. If you are changing your approach for cycle 2, state it here.)

Figure 3.1 *Continued.*

Step #	Cycle 2 detailed steps	Person(s) responsible	Measure/ indicator	Start date	End date
#1					

Deployment Plan Quality Check:

What resources/budget needs do you have for cycle 2?

If you identified budget needs, what budget code will you use to meet the budget needs for this cycle?

If funding is not available, list the steps from the deployment plan that will address the funding gap.

What professional development, if any, will be offered in cycle 2 to support the staff in implementing the approach?

Determine the measures/data that will be used to determine the effectiveness of the cycle 2 approach by answering the following questions:

A. What data will you use to determine if the approach was deployed?	B. What data will you use to determine if the approach was deployed with fidelity?	C. What data will you use to determine if the approach impacted the overall goal or target goal?

S	Study: Analysis of data after implementing approach.

At the end of cycle 2, answer the following questions based on the data collected from your identified measures:

1. What are the key strengths and data to support them?	2. What are the key opportunities for improvement and the data to support them?	3. What information/data are needed that we do not have?

Reflect on the data analysis for cycle 2. Which option best describes your direction for cycle 3?

☐ Target goal has been met and is changed to reflect new target. ☐ Target goal not met, but data indicates current approach is effective so we will continue current approach and repeat deployment plan for the next cycle.	☐ Target goal not met so we will continue current approach but make improvements to deployment plan based on data analysis above. ☐ Target goal not met, and data indicates gap is widening so we will abandon current approach and identify a new approach.

Figure 3.1 *Continued.*

A	Act: Revise or continue with deployment plan based on data analysis.

4. What is your next step for cycle 3? Identify key approach or strategy. (If you are continuing with the approach from cycle 2, restate it here. If you are changing your approach for cycle 3, state it here.)

Step #	Cycle 3 detailed steps	Person(s) responsible	Measure/ indicator	Start date	End date
#1					

Deployment Plan Quality Check:

What resources/budget needs do you have for cycle 3?

If you identified budget needs, what budget code will you use to meet the budget needs for this cycle?

If funding is not available, list the steps from the deployment plan that will address the funding gap.

What professional development, if any, will be offered in cycle 3 to support the staff in implementing the approach?

Determine the measures/data that will be used to determine the effectiveness of the cycle 3 approach by answering the following questions:

A. What data will you use to determine if the approach was deployed?	B. What data will you use to determine if the approach was deployed with fidelity?	C. What data will you use to determine if the approach impacted the overall goal or target goal?

S	Study: Analysis of data after implementing a strategy.

At the end of cycle 3, answer the following questions based on the data collected from your identified measures:

1. What are the key strengths and data to support them?	2. What are the key opportunities for improvement and the data to support them?	3. What information/data are needed that we do not have?

Figure 3.1 *Continued.*

Reflect on the data analysis for cycle 3. Which option best describes your direction for cycle 4?	
☐ Target goal has been met and is changed to reflect new target. ☐ Target goal not met, but data indicates current approach is effective so we will continue current approach and repeat deployment plan for the next cycle.	☐ Target goal not met so we will continue current approach but make improvements to deployment plan based on data analysis above. ☐ Target goal not met, and data indicates gap is widening so we will abandon current approach and identify a new approach.

A	Act: Revise or continue with deployment plan based on data analysis.

4. What is your next step for cycle 4? Identify key approach or strategy. (If you are continuing with the approach from cycle 3, restate it here. If you are changing your approach for cycle 4, state it here.)

Step #	Cycle 4 detailed steps	Person(s) responsible	Measure/ indicator	Start date	End date
#1					

Deployment Plan Quality Check:

What resources/budget needs do you have for cycle 4?

If you identified budget needs, what budget code will you use to meet the budget needs for this cycle?

If funding is not available, list the steps from the deployment plan that will address the funding gap.

What professional development, if any, will be offered in cycle 4 to support the staff in implementing the approach?

Determine the measures/data that will be used to determine the effectiveness of the cycle 4 approach by answering the following questions:

A. What data will you use to determine if the approach was deployed?	B. What data will you use to determine if the approach was deployed with fidelity?	C. What data will you use to determine if the approach impacted the overall goal or target goal?

Figure 3.1 *Continued.*

decisions made in planning at all levels. We were able to create a consistent approach to school improvement planning, and the changes needed to deploy the plan are beginning to happen.

CONNECTING TO RESEARCH

Kotter (2008) calls this "bringing the outside in"; however, he cautions that outside consultants are often not successful in moving the organization forward. They bring information and knowledge into the district but often the knowledge gained does not translate into workplace application.

I mentioned earlier in Chapter 2 that my relationship with Terry Holliday became one of coach, mentor, ruthlessly compassionate friend, and coworker. With the exception of coworker, I experienced this relationship with four other clients and, where this type of relationship developed, I was able to be a positive force in helping those districts change their cultures to accomplish their visions. Terry worked with me and spent a lot of time preparing me for what I needed to do, rather than hiring me to come in and "stand and deliver" content. Each session was focused on what the middle management leaders needed to know in order to do the next level of work for the district.

Research suggests that you must change the behavior of the people in the organization before you can change the culture. The behavior has to become a habit before the culture can be transformed. Kotter (2008) indicates that changes "in norms and shared values come at the end of the transformation process," and that data reporting positive movement is essential to convincing people that the approach will work. For us, creating a data system that reported comparisons of student attendance across the district, then publishing that data monthly, was important, but we had to go further. We also built in monthly conversations with principals based on the data, and that finally was the key piece in changing the district culture to one that embraces continual improvement.

A FOCUS ON RESULTS

Shifting to a template approach to school improvement planning, and creating a consistent, definable, repeatable, predictable process to support the development and deployment of those plans, caused behaviors to change. While it was a three-year journey from the first poorly worded goals to a working school improvement plan, this planning process is now the way we do our work.

The SIP process was designed to create a PDSA of the deployment plans in the SIP every nine weeks. At that time, the school leadership team received a one-hour review/coaching session focused on strengths of their work, opportunities for improvement, support needed from the district, and next steps. A summary feedback report is delivered, via e-mail, to the school leadership team by the end of the day of coaching so they can share the input with their staff. (See Figure 3.2 for an example of a feedback report.) From these coaching sessions, information was gathered that guided the allocation of district resources, professional development support, district department assistance, and budgeting of monies to support school initiatives.

School Improvement Plan Coaching/Feedback Report	
School: Home Town Elementary	**Quarter:** 3/4
Date of SIP review: 4/29/09	**In attendance:** Principal, instructional facilitator, executive director of elementary education, chief quality officer, reading and math goal team leaders.

Strengths:
- Reading goal team did an excellent job with identifying and collecting data on fidelity of implementation of their strategy, determining opportunities for improvement (OFIs), and creating a deployment plan to address the OFIs.
- Principal gives much credit to instructional facilitator for the knowledge and coaching she has brought to the SIP process.
- School has created an Intervention Fidelity Observation Instrument through PLCs to observe HYIS implementation.
- Reading PDSA at classroom level and reading small group instruction has been implemented with focus on fidelity to ensure high level of implementation. Groups are meeting two times per week for 30 minutes.
- Some teachers are now doing two classroom PDSAs plus a PLC PDSA.
- Most PDSAs are current now and IF/AP and principal have a process to follow up if teachers are having problems meeting expectations.
- Reading data is up in all grade levels with exception of first grade. First grade scored at the same level on DRA two cycles in a row . . . 75th percentile.
- Math tutoring sessions are occurring two times a week for 45 minutes with struggling students. Tutored students are showing good gains beyond the non-tutored group.

Figure 3.2   SIP coaching/feedback report example.   *Continued*

- Principal and IF/AP do walk-throughs to observe interventions based on schedule.
- Professional development was provided for teachers on guided reading for the intervention groups.
- Cooperative learning is more prevalent across all grade levels.
- Leadership team meets weekly and shares minutes transparently with staff.
- There is a clearly defined communication process, goal team Report-Out Sheets, to monitor and support goal teams.
- Principal and IF/AP have L to J process to randomly review lesson plans by grade level and provide feedback. Principal credits IF with strength of process.
- Principal attends PD and is attempting to get into more and more PLCs.
- PBS has been established as a PDSA schoolwide instead of a SIP goal, and team members are functioning better as an organized team.
- Computer test scores are highest in district.
- Student at Home Town Elementary wrote a book and won first place at state level.
- AIG fifth grade were only group to show growth in district for reading.

Opportunities for improvement:

- While Guided Reading is being implemented, additional work can be focused on fidelity of implementation at this point.
- First grade made no gains in reading or math from second to third quarter on PAs.
- HYIS implementation is at about 50% in math and reading, and additional professional development and buy-in is needed for/by staff.
- Principal should continue to expand time in PLCs where possible.

Suggested action step(s):

- Transfer knowledge gained in reading on fidelity of implementation of key strategies to the work of the math goal team.
- First grade should review instructional practice as a team and look at best practices of other grade level teams that have made significant growth and determine if application in first grade would benefit student learning.
- Continue setting high expectations for HYIS and provide professional development in areas needed as defined by fidelity instrument.
- Contact district grant writer and ask her to look for possible grants to expand the Guided Reading materials.

Area(s) of focus before next review:

- First grade coaching and support should be an ongoing focus for the leadership team.

Resources/needs from district

- Additional Guided Reading materials are needed.

Figure 3.2 *Continued.*

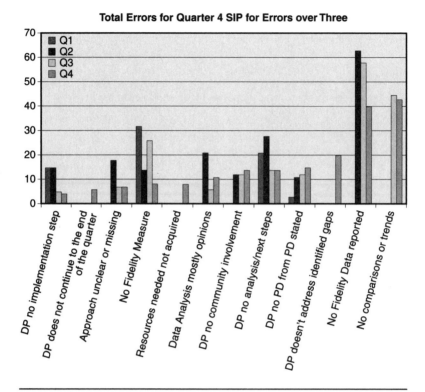

Figure 3.3 SIP template error frequency rate.

The result of the coaching and feedback provided to school leadership teams as they developed and deployed their school improvement plans resulted in higher performance in the area of strategic planning as is evidenced by the chart in Figure 3.3.

The increased ability of school and district department teams to be able to focus on gap identification and to put plans in place that engaged their staff in doing the right work in the right areas resulted in increased district performance in all key areas. Highlights of this turnaround performance are detailed in Table 3.1.

Table 3.1   Iredell–Statesville Schools turnaround highlights.

Measure	2002 results	2008 results	Process improvement
Graduation rate	61% 53rd in NC	81% 11th in NC	Dropout prevention plan
SAT	991 57th in NC	1056 Seventh in NC	SAT plan–do–study–act
3–8 Reading	77% proficient 75th in NC	90% proficient Top 20 in NC	Read 180
3–8 Math	68th in NC	12th in NC	Continuous improvement model
3–8 Reading gap for African American	23 percentage points	12 percentage points	School improvement plans
3–8 Reading gap for exceptional children	43 percentage points	20 percentage points	Corrective reading
Computer skills test	68% proficient	90% proficient	Computer skills plan–do–study–act
Dropout rate	6.5%	3.8%	Dropout prevention plan
Attendance rate	94.1% 55th in NC	96.1% Third in NC	Attendance plan–do–study–act
Out of school suspension	Over 3500 days	Reduced by 50%	Positive behavior support
Bus discipline incidents	Over 3200 referrals	Less than 1600 referrals	Positive behavior support
Out of school suspension days saved	0	Over 3800	Out of school suspension reporting center
Business partners	40	185	Golden opportunities plan–do–study–act
Faith-based partners	0	64	Closing the Gap Committee
Parent conferences	65%	95%	School improvement plans

Continued

Table 3.1 *Continued.*

Measure	2002 results	2008 results	Process improvement
High school credit recovery	500 courses	Over 2100 courses	School improvement plans
Operating fund balance	−$2.5 million	$4 million	Funding plan–do–study–act
Energy savings	0	Over $4 million	Energy education
External audit findings	11	Zero for last five years	Finance plan–do–study–act
Highly qualified teachers	80%	95%	Recruitment and retention plan–do–study–act
National board certified teachers	6%	10%	Recruitment and retention plan–do–study–act
Worker's Compensation loss ratio	132.31	3.49	Safety Committee plan–do–study–act
Baldrige National Quality Program review score	83	626 Among top 6% of all applicants	BNQP Criteria
Expenditures per pupil	Bottom 10 in NC	Bottom 10 in NC	Zero-based budgeting

4

Red Light #4—District Leadership and Governance

by Terry Holliday

It was an important turning point in our journey. I will never forget the board of education meeting where we discovered we had run through a red light and we needed to back up a little. We were about three years into our journey to turn around the school system. For the first two years, we had picked the low-hanging fruit. We had implemented the I–SS *raising achievement and closing gaps model* (see Figure 4.1) in our Title I schools.

We had implemented aligned strategic plans between the district, departments, and schools. Our early successes had led us to expand the model to all schools during the third year of operation. We were basically trying to break the molds. As any superintendent who implements a change in direction for a school system knows, you will occasionally run through

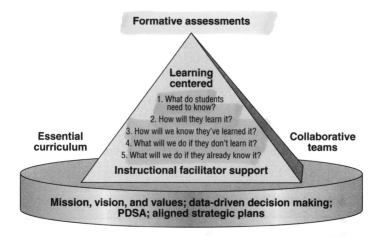

Figure 4.1 I–SS model to raise achievement and close gaps.

a red light and be forced to back up and possibly change direction. We had tried to run a few red lights and we were not certain we had the support or sense of urgency to run those lights. A red light we had been running was the lack of principal leadership in addressing teacher concerns with the I–SS model. We thought we could run a few red lights due to our early successes and we were emboldened by them. We were not prepared for how the red light manifested itself. Teachers and staff were lobbying school board members directly for relief of what they saw as too much paperwork, too many meetings, and too much intrusion of the school system into what happens in classrooms. The only way that we could continue in our general direction of success for all students was with the support of the board of education. All too often, a school superintendent and the direction of the school system are stopped completely by a board of education that is not supportive of the direction of the change initiative. As it turned out, we were able to back up at the red light due to our preparation of governance and district leadership and the board's overall support of our model. I am often asked by superintendents how we were successful in implementing the change and achieving the results we have obtained. The success would not have been possible without the full support of the school board. How did we get that support and prepare the board for the challenges that would surely come when a change initiative is implemented? That is the story . . . .

THE STORY: SCHOOL BOARD— GOVERNANCE DEVELOPMENT

When I interviewed for the superintendent position at Iredell–Statesville, the board seemed interested in how I had used the Baldrige Criteria in my current superintendent position to improve the school system. The I–SS board emphasized a desire to become a top-performing school system in North Carolina, and I told them that I believed a systemic and systematic approach to continuous improvement contained within the Baldrige Criteria could be used to lead the school system to that vision. The board eventually was unanimous in their support of me and the use of the Baldrige Criteria as the management and leadership criteria for the turnaround of the school system. Reflecting back on our trip, I believe there were several key pieces to our journey:

1. From the beginning, it is extremely important that the superintendent and school board have an understanding and agreement on direction and destination for the school system (vision and mission).

2. The board and superintendent must agree on the road map for getting to the destination (strategic plan and continuous improvement model).

3. The superintendent must model the behaviors that will be expected of the board and all staff for the change journey.

4. The board must model the behaviors that will be expected of the staff for the change journey.

5. The district must have a management process that focuses on accountability for results expected from the plan.

In Chapter 1, I talked about the listening tour and the three questions that drove the early work in the school system. Not only did this tour serve the purpose of modeling for principals and teachers what a continuous improvement focus would look like, it also modeled the process for the board of education. Typically, a school board does not completely understand their roles and responsibilities. Too often, school boards respond to the latest phone call or anonymous letter that they have received from their constituents rather than rely on qualitative or quantitative data. What I did with the listening tour was to model a method to gain qualitative data and then develop priorities for improvement so the board could make data-driven decisions about which change priorities to pursue. The board had never been engaged in this type of collaborative process. It was very much new learning for them. During the process, I had asked the board to answer the same three questions that the staff and community had responded to in the listening tour. I then had the board, staff, and community rank the priorities that needed to be addressed. The board was then able to see what the top priorities were for each of the three questions. When it became obvious that the staff felt student attendance needed to be addressed since it was a major barrier in helping students be more successful, it was not difficult to get the board to adopt a policy change for student attendance. Then, as the policy was deployed and board members began to receive complaints from individual parents about the new policy and implementation of the policy, the board was able to fall back on the data from the listening tour, which had clearly established the need for improvement in student attendance data. This was the beginning of board training and coaching that enabled the board to stay at the policy and governance level rather than the implementation level of the school system.

After the early success of the attendance policy change, toward the end of the first year, the board began to make explicit changes in the way they did business. The first change was in the development of a budget for the school system. In previous years, the board had been very involved in the detail level of the budget. Not only did the board look at specific functions of the budget, the board looked closely at detailed line items of the budget. Board members described the process as very labor-intensive and very exhausting on their part. The board was open to a change in the process that allowed them to set the priorities and then allow the administration to develop the details. I introduced the board to a zero-based budget process. I had developed a level of trust with the board through the first year by reducing expenditures and balancing a budget that was initially $2 million over budget for available revenues. Also, the initial success of a PDSA in improving school attendance helped the board develop confidence in the use of Baldrige Criteria for management and leadership. The zero-based budget process is described in Appendix A. The major steps included:

1. Presentation by all budget owners from a zero-based perspective rather than simply asking for expansion items or redirection of existing budget resources.

2. Each budget owner had to show how every budget expenditure was aligned to the North Carolina State Board strategic plan.

3. Each budget owner had to show how expenditures were aligned to raising achievement and closing gaps, or making support processes more efficient and effective.

The first year of the process was very challenging. We had a budget committee comprising the superintendent, finance officer, principals representing each grade level, and the human resource director. The age of transparency had finally arrived. Many budget owners had control of budgets of which principals and other central office departments had little knowledge. The first budget line item accounting was done for the central office budget that the superintendent controlled. As superintendent, I showed the budget committee concrete reductions in the superintendent's budget of over $500,000. Leading by example was crucial for success of the budget process. As we continued, the principals on the committee kept the other principals from their grade level informed and received feedback from the other principals on what questions needed to be asked of budget owners. Eventually, we were able to identify expansion items (most of these had come from my listening tour results for question #2—"what do you need to help more children be successful") and the redirection of dollars from the existing budget (over $2 million). We then did something totally unheard of in the system. We asked the teachers and staff to rank budget expansion items. Of course, the teachers and staff recognized many of the expansion items from the listening tour responses to question #2 that they had provided.

That was when I got the comments—"If we had known you were actually going to listen to our comments and do something about them we would have been more reflective in our responses." When we received the survey results that prioritized budget expansion items, we allowed the principals one final shot at prioritizing budget expansion and redirection items. When we took the budget to the board for the public hearing, board budget work sessions, and final approval, the entire involvement of the board was less than six hours as compared to over 40 hours in previous years. The board learned about transparency and systematic processes through the just-in-time training on the zero-based budget process. Coupling the success of the attendance PDSA with the budget PDSA, we had the early successes that we needed to continue our work in implementing the Baldrige Criteria within the system.

At the end of the first year, we had a board work session to review our progress as a school system. Three months prior to the work session, we had taken the existing strategic plan for the school system and had worked with principals, departments, and the community to draft revisions to the existing strategic plan. The original strategic plan for the school district filled a notebook, and very few of the principals were aware of the goals of the strategic plan, and even fewer had any idea how their school improvement plan should be aligned to the district strategic plan. In fact, most school improvement plans were in notebooks that the principal and leadership team had developed and then sat on a shelf until the next plan was due. In Chapter 3, we discussed the level of work we were doing to show principals and departments the importance of aligned strategic plans.

Our challenge was creating a district strategic plan that was practical and doable. The development of the district strategic plan was very much paper driven; however, we had an excellent example from the North Carolina State Board of Education. We established area advisory meetings where we invited parents, community, and staff members to attend and give feedback about the strategic priorities for the school system. The strategic priorities for the state were:

1. High student performance

2. Healthy, safe, orderly, and caring schools

3. Quality teachers and staff

4. Partnerships with parents and community

5. Effective and efficient operations

At the area advisory meetings, we asked the participants to respond to several questions:

1. Are these the right priorities for our school system?

2. What would be possible measures for each priority?

3. Do we have data for the measures?

4. If we have the data, how are we doing in comparison to state and other school systems similar to ours?

We utilized the same process that we had used with the listening tour questions. We affinitized all responses and then sent the list of possible measures back to all participants to rank. We then pulled in principals and district leaders to review the community and staff feedback and to finalize the strategic priorities and goals for the district strategic plan. We brought to the school board a revised three-page strategic plan that was directly aligned to the North Carolina State Board of Education ABC strategic plan. The proposed strategic plan had 35 goals aligned with the five strategic priorities for North Carolina. All of the 35 goals were SMART goals with one-year and three-year horizons for performance. A key for the plan was that the board was asked only to establish goals, not develop strategies or deployment plans. Deployment is the work of the departments and the schools. Keeping the board at this level is crucial. We continue today in this vein. The board approves changes to goals and indicators. The board either accepts or rejects a department or school improvement plan that contains strategies and deployment. The board does not micromanage improvement strategies or deployment plans.

The importance of a district strategic plan that is widely communicated to all stakeholders can not be overstated. However, perhaps the most important learning for us was that the strategic plan belonged to the board of education and the school system. It was not the superintendent's strategic plan. It was not a plan developed by the director of strategic planning. It was a plan developed by the board based on feedback from all stakeholders.

From this early strategic plan came the measures to which we would hold all principals and department heads accountable for performance in our leadership evaluation and coaching process. The five strategic priorities and 35 measures became our balanced scorecard by which we let the community know how well we were performing and how close we were to reaching our vision and mission. The board continues to model the importance of the strategic plan by conducting midyear and end-of-year review sessions of progress on the strategic plan. At these midyear and end-of-year sessions, staff members present a SWOT (strengths, weaknesses, opportunities for improvement, and threats) analysis for each of the strategic priorities. The *strengths* list the major accomplishments of goals and successes on leading indicators that impact the district goals. The *weaknesses* list where the school system has not achieved the goal or the leading indi-cators that might predict we will not reach our goal. The *opportunities for improvement* reporting section lists those district processes that need to be improved to impact the results from lagging or leading indicators. Finally, the *threats* reporting section lists those external issues that the board needs to consider that could have a positive or negative influence on the capacity of the school system to reach the strategic goals and priorities.

While the strategic plan with strategic priorities and strategic goals was an important document, the *most important* outcome of the board work session at the end of the first year was the adoption of a district vision to become a "top ten performing school system in North Carolina." We set timelines to perform above state average within three years, perform above regional comparisons within five years, and perform at or above top ten level within seven years. Having a vision that everyone could understand, state, and relate to their work was essential for our success as a school system in implementing a strategic plan and a continuous improvement approach.

A couple of other significant outcomes came from the board work sessions in the second and third years. In 2004–05 we trained the board on a systems check provided by Jim Shipley & Associates. This systems check was basically a board of education self-assessment of how well the board was performing as measured against the Baldrige Criteria. Also, the systems check had a survey component that allowed the board's stake-holders to inform the board on how well the board was performing. The board had never done a self-assessment. Several board members felt that the only real evaluation of a board member was the public election held every two years. Thanks to strong leadership from the board chair and encouragement from the superintendent that the board should model what they expected from all schools and departments, the board agreed to the self-assessment and survey.

The system check results were difficult for some of the board members to accept. The survey ratings from stakeholders were difficult for some board members to accept. The discussions around the results revealed some misinformation and misunderstandings about the role of the board as spelled out in board policies. However, having the systems check and sur-vey results was powerful in that it was not the superintendent or a consul-tant telling the board how it could improve; it was the stakeholders telling the board how to improve. The final outcome was the board of education improvement plan (Figure 4.3) that is updated annually and the board of education described as a system (Figure 4.2). Over the course of the last five years, the board has conducted the semiannual performance reviews of the school system and reviews of the progress of the board on the systems check, stakeholder survey, and board improvement plan goals, all of this guided against the Baldrige Criteria expressed in the board of education systems chart. The I–SS board has been recognized at the state level for an innovative approach to board improvement and has been recognized by several site visit teams from Baldrige and the Southern Association of Colleges and Schools for their innovative approach to board improvement. The evidences of the board actually doing what it was expecting from schools and departments had a major impact on the buy-in from principals and department heads and eventually teachers.

CONNECTING TO RESEARCH

As a superintendent, you learn very quickly that the red lights will come quickly once you begin to implement change in a school system. The more change you expect at the school and classroom level, the quicker you will see the red lights. As superintendent, you must be prepared to change direction at the red light, back up in case you have gone beyond the red light, or run the red light. The only way you can run the light is with authority from the board and a sense of urgency that if you do not run the red light, students and staff will suffer. As a superintendent, you quickly learn that a very important ability is the ability to count to four, five, or whatever number represents a majority of the board. While children and learning are certainly our focus and our purpose, our primary customer has to be the board of education members. If you do not have a level of satisfaction with this customer group, you do not have a job very long as a superintendent. A superintendent must keep the board well informed and must provide coaching, training, and support over time for board members. If a board does not approve a recommendation from the superintendent, it could be due to lack of preparation and information from the superintendent. A level of trust and confidence must be present between board members and superintendent.

School, state, or national systemic reform of education is very difficult to achieve. Michael Fullan in *Turnaround Leadership* (2006) discusses the enormous challenges in changing a school system to achieve improved results. Dr. Fullan cites an analysis of systemic reform efforts from three large school systems in Chicago, Milwaukee, and Seattle. These three systems had change efforts focused on additional dollars for improving literacy and math, implementing choice options, concentrating on assessment, focusing professional development, changing leadership, and changing the system. The conclusion of the study (Cross City Campaign for Urban School Reform) was the unfortunate reality for principals and teachers that the districts were unable to change and improve practice on a large scale.

While there were many surface changes (choice, leadership, and assessment) there were very few deep changes at the level that matters most—the classroom. Many writers compare this to a major storm at sea. While the waves may be large and there is significant turbulence at the surface level, the bottom of the ocean remains quite calm and undisturbed. Teachers often say it like this—"I have seen many superintendents and change initiatives come and go and I have outlasted all of them. Just leave me alone and let me do what I have always done." Of course, this would be fine if students in large numbers had been successful. However, in many cases the inequity between classroom teachers in the same school on student learning outcomes is not only a matter of fact, but also in the perceptions of parents, who will go to great lengths to avoid specific teachers. The level of commitment of the governance and the district leadership in a system is very important; however, it alone is not sufficient. There must be deep change in leadership practices at the school and classroom levels. If your governance board and your district leadership are not ready for the criticism and efforts to abandon change that will surely come, then the change initiative will fail. In our case, we had prepared the board of education through practical application at the district level of the changes we would be expecting at the classroom level. The Baldrige Criteria are appropriate at any level of an organization. What we did in I–SS was to translate the Baldrige Criteria with the help of Jim Shipley & Associates into language that every level of the organization could understand, we implemented processes requiring the deployment of the Criteria, we held *everyone* accountable for implementing the reforms, and we constantly revised our expectations based on the results we were obtaining.

Michael Fullan in *Turnaround Leadership* (2006) discusses several examples of how a school system can turn around and achieve success for children. The York Region School District just north of Toronto is one example. It is a rapidly growing system with a total of 170 schools. The reform efforts have been ongoing since 2001 and are focused in a district plan called the Literacy Collaborative. The plan has five basic components:

1. Clearly articulated vision and commitment to success for all children

2. Systemwide plan and framework for continuous improvement

3. The use of data to drive improvement in instruction and alignment of resources

4. Capacity building at the principal and teacher level

5. Implementation of professional learning communities at all levels

The I–SS model for raising achievement and closing gaps connected to the district strategic plan and district vision is almost a carbon copy of these five components (see Figure 4.1 above).

Dr. Fullan continues in his book by showing the connection from the local board level to the state and national level. Dr. Fullan connects England's National Literacy and Numeracy Strategy from 1999–2002 with the current Ontario systemic reform. While the reform efforts differ slightly in strategy, one common component is in leadership and governance. In Ontario, the premier of Ontario, Dalton McGuinty, provided the leadership and governance support to initiate systemic reform in education. In England, the prime minister and minister of education provided the governance and leadership (Tony Blair and David Blunkett). In both cases of systemic reform, the results have been impressive.

Robert Marzano, in *District Leadership That Works* (2009), provided further evidence that the I–SS approach is aligned to research. In a meta-analysis of 27 studies that included results from 2817 school districts representing 3.4 million students, Marzano reports a positive correlation between student learning and district leadership. This is further described in the McKinsey report *How the World's Best-Performing School Systems Come Out on Top* (2007) that studies the top-performing school systems in the world. The McKinsey report found no systemic reform efforts leading to improved student outcomes without the presence of strong district or system leadership committed to change and improved learning for *all* students.

Marzano (2009) listed several key strategies that successful district leaders used when implementing change that resulted in improved student outcomes. The first of these was a focus on goals. This focus on goals is described as a process of collaborative goal setting, nonnegotiable learning goals, alignment between board of education strategic plan and school improvement plans, alignment of resources to accomplish plans, close monitoring of goals, and the use of resources to support achievement and improve instruction. As the first few chapters of this book have evidenced, the I–SS model included an early focus on collaboration with stakeholders by involving the entire staff in the initial needs assessment and then the involvement of all stakeholders in development of the district strategic plan. The board of education, through the adoption of a strategic plan and a vision statement focused on student learning, revealed to all stakeholders the nonnegotiable learning goals and board alignment and support.

In his book *Leadership for Results* (2006), Tom Barker discusses how to remove barriers to success. His focus on intentions, information, and influence of leadership is also represented in the I–SS approach. Barker focuses on intentions first. He recommends that an organization identify stakeholder needs and expectations and feed the information into development of a purpose for the organization, ensure that the purpose drives the work of everyone in the organization, and make certain that the purpose answers three key questions—Do what? For whom? How? Those three questions served as the model for development of our mission statements during the community meetings to develop our strategic plan. We train all levels in our school system to use the same three questions when developing a school, department, or classroom mission.

Barker then talks about translating intentions into action. My father-in-law, who is a minister, often says the "road to hell is paved with good intentions." In other words, words without deeds are useless. One of our favorite statements when doing staff training is "theory without action is useless and action not based on theory can be very costly." Barker states that actions define purpose more than a mission statement could ever do. These actions should include the involvement of staff in refining the purpose through alignment of work. Leaders should discuss purpose at every opportunity—not only when faced with dissent or resistance but in every meeting or discussion.

Finally, leadership should focus on essential actions that are aligned to the purpose and identify actions to abandon that are not aligned. In our school system we call this purposeful abandonment. Quite often, it is more important for district leaders and governance to focus on what they are going to quit doing rather than what they will do. By changing the budget process, strategic planning process, and attendance process in our school system, the board of education signaled several things that they would quit doing. They would quit spending hours of fruitless discussion on line item budgets and spend more time on the purpose and expected learning outcomes. In that way, expenditures could be more closely monitored for alignment to expectations for student results. By adopting a three-year strategic plan, the board moved from a monthly reaction to the latest stakeholder complaints to a strategic focus on learning outcomes and the vision and mission of the school system. By adopting a clear and guiding policy related to attendance, the board signaled a change in the level of support for classroom teachers who identified student attendance as a major barrier to learning outcomes. Clearly, a focus by governance and leadership of a school system on intentions and purpose will drive improvement in results.

Barker next focuses on information. He encourages leadership to promote fact-based decisions based on stakeholder needs and expectations, identify conclusions from data analysis that address stakeholder risks and needs, and align decisions and actions with stakeholder needs and expectations in mind. The I–SS board of education clearly followed these guidelines in the development of the mission, vision, and strategic plan for the school system.

Finally, Barker discusses the key strategy of influence. Barker encourages a focus on give and take and a focus on a win/win strategy. He recommends that leaders identify ground rules that govern behavior of teams within the organization:

- Give and take with yourself—focus on things you can influence and do not focus on things you can not influence.

- Give and take with your team—focus on outcomes of student learning rather than focusing on things that make you as an individual look good.

- Give and take with your boss—seek understanding of the reasoning behind assignments from your boss and seek win/win for your boss and the organization.

- Promote stakeholder thinking—always come back to a focus on stakeholder needs and expectations.

- Stop doing a "to do" list—create a list of things that you will stop doing versus those things you will do.

- Align results with purpose—always align the results of improvements with the purpose of the organization.

- Write down what you expect to happen.

- Share data with teams and stakeholders.

As the I–SS board of education moved from a reactionary board to a strategic and systemic board, all of these elements were present.

The red light of governance and district leadership must be addressed and, as we have shown, it can be addressed. If we had not addressed this governance and district leadership red light, we would not have been able to survive the red lights that appeared from staff members. Let me repeat that: if we had not addressed this governance and district leadership red light, we would not have been able to survive the red lights that appeared from staff members. We will now show the types of processes for data-driven decision making, focused results, and written plans that helped us enable a school board to support the change that led a system to achieve outstanding learning and operations results.

A FOCUS ON RESULTS

In order to encourage change that will improve student learning outcomes, it is important for leadership and governance to model the change that is expected. The I–SS board of education adopted a governance model based on the categories of the Baldrige performance management system. Figure 4.2 describes this model.

During monthly board meetings and semiannual board work sessions, the superintendent focuses the board of education training and coaching on this model. During the semiannual work sessions, the board does a self-assessment of progress toward board of education goals and a self-assessment of each of the Baldrige Criteria items using a systems check developed by Jim Shipley & Associates. Figure 4.3 shows the board of education improvement plan that is one result of these semiannual reviews.

The actual board survey and results for the last four years are shown in Figure 4.4.

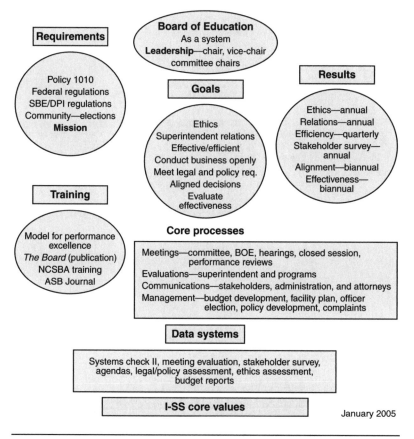

Figure 4.2 I–SS board of education governance model.

I-SS Board of Education Improvement Plan
2008–09 School Year

Board goal Target goal	Measure	Action step	Responsible	Timeline
Maintain effective relations with superintendent and staff	Survey item #2	Attend area advisory rezoning meetings	Partnerships coordinator	September 2008 February 2009
• Improve results on item #2 to 75%		Scheduled visits to schools with superintendent	Administrative assistant	TBD
		Ratings of superintendent communications	Administrative assistant	March 2009
Operate cost-effectively and efficiently	Survey item #14 % of phase II completed	Complete phase II facilities plan	Superintendent	August 2009
• Improve results on item #14 to 75%		Identify $3M in budget cuts revenue	Director of construction	January 2009
			Superintendent	
• 100% of phase II construction on time and within budget				
Meet legal and policy requirements	Compliance with NCGS 115C-50	Midyear and end-of-year reviews	Superintendent	March and August 2008
• Every board member shall receive a minimum of 12 clock hours of training relevant to the I–SS strategic goals and the BOE improvement goals		Attend NCSBA regional meetings	Administrative assistant	September 2008
		Attend NCSBA conferences	Administrative assistant	As scheduled
		PDSA training	Associate superintendent	TBA

Continued

Figure 4.3 Board of education overall and target goals with action steps.

**I-SS Board of Education Improvement Plan
2008–09 School Year**

Board goal Target goal	Measure	Action step	Responsible	Timeline
Periodically evaluate board effectiveness	Composite of survey items #8, 9, 10	Document PDSA steps on board agenda items	Superintendent	Monthly
• Improve results on composite of survey items #8, 9, 10 to 80%	Community survey SC3	Report BOE progress on improvement plan quarterly	Superintendent	November, February, April, August
• Achieve 75% A/B rating on community survey	Plan and funding plan	Continue implementing community satisfaction survey	Director of public relations	November 2008
• Develop phase III facilities plan and obtain funding from Iredell County commissioners		Eliminate "no opinion" from BOE survey	Chief accountability and technology officer	February 2009
		Utilize stakeholder response rate used by comparative district phase III meetings	Superintendent	August 2008– March 2009
		Joint Finance Committee meeting	Superintendent	March 2009

Figure 4.3 *Continued*

Item	Agreement 04–05	Agreement 05–06	Agreement 06–07	Agreement 07–08	Comparison district 06–07
The board of education works with the superintendent and staff in a climate of professionalism and mutual respect	59.6	85.0	86.9	98.6	97.0
Board of education members communicate with district staff using approved procedure	68.3	65.6	69.4	90.3	86.0
The board of education has adopted and practices the board of education code of ethics	80.0	91.5	84.3	100.0	95.0
The board of education exhibits ethics, integrity, flexibility, and tact when working as a board	86.7	91.7	85.5	98.6	93.0
The board of education supports the superintendent and district in using a systems approach to continuous improvement to improve departments, schools, and classrooms	93.3	91.7	87.1	97.3	100.0
The board of education is accessible and responsive to the superintendent, staff, and other stakeholders	76.7	43.9	84.0	92.9	97.0
Board members use the district process and chain of command to resolve problems and complaints	76.3	75.0	80.2	90.6	85.0
The board of education works as a team in leading the district	81.4	76.3	73.9	92.8	97.0

Continued

Figure 4.4   Survey results from board of education climate survey received from district employees and key stakeholders.

Item	Agreement 04–05	Agreement 05–06	Agreement 06–07	Agreement 07–08	Comparison district 06–07
The board of education makes decisions to support the district priorities and not individual board member agendas	53.1	81.4	74.7	92.8	76.0
The board of education builds and maintains relationships with other governmental agencies	65.0	72.4	72.3	76.6	89.0
The board of education builds and maintains relationships with the community	59.5	49.8	83.2	95.5	85.0
The board of education incorporates core values (best practices) in board operations	85.0	79.7	80.0	97.1	96.0
The board of education demonstrates fiscal responsibility in management of the budget	63.6	96.6	89.4	98.6	94.0
The board of education provides for adequate district facilities	40.5	45.8	74.4	76.1	84.0
Average of all questions	70.64	74.72	80.38	92.70	91

Figure 4.4 *Continued.*

Through a focus on stakeholder expectations and comparison with a high-performing school system that also utilizes the Baldrige Criteria, the board of education has modeled the continuous improvement focus expected of all levels of the school system. Clearly, the board of education has modeled intentions, information, and influence through a systems approach to performance excellence.

The board of education does not rely solely on internal assessments or surveys of stakeholders. Through application to the North Carolina Awards for Excellence and the Baldrige National Quality Program, the I–SS board of education has received external validation of their leadership and governance practices. Figure 4.5 shows the results from these external reviews.

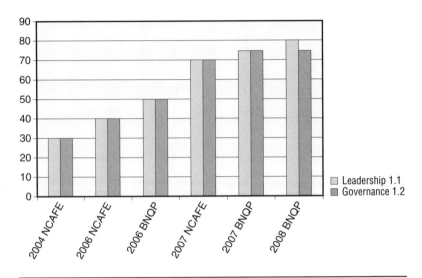

Figure 4.5 External review for I–SS on leadership and governance items.

Additionally, I–SS became one of the first 30 school systems in the nation to receive recognition as a Quality School System by the Southern Association of Colleges and Schools in 2006. Also, I–SS was among the first school systems in the nation to achieve this accreditation as a district by using the Baldrige Criteria.

This chapter started with the recounting of a pivotal moment in the history of our school system. As system leaders, we had done good work in preparing our school board for what to expect as we moved through the change process required when implementing a new model of leadership and management. Our work had been modeled after the research of Fullan, Reeves, Barker, Marzano, and others. We had experienced early successes, and we were passionate about the need to change all of our schools so all children could be successful. However, we had almost made a fatal mistake. We had run a red light and we did not quite have the sense of urgency or the legal authority to run it. The red light was the lack of school-level leadership capacity to address the concerns of teachers and staff that were resistant to the change. The teachers and staff were resistant due to complacency and a myriad of other reasons. However, we knew that unless we equipped principals and building leadership with the capacity to lead change, our efforts to achieve success for all children were doomed. Chapter 5 will describe our efforts and the results from those efforts.

5

Red Light #5—Leadership Capacity to Do the Work

by Brenda Clark

In the previous chapter, the importance of board of education leadership was outlined. Professional development for the board is critical in building a high-performing team that recognizes its responsibility for setting clear direction and expectations without micromanaging schools, district departments, and, most importantly, the superintendent. Creating a common purpose and clear understanding of the role of the board is critical to high performance in the district.

When the board fully understands the performance data of the district and endorses the strategic direction, a major red light for the schools turns to green. With a green light you have the euphoric feeling that you can charge ahead, but this should be a time of caution. As Terry stated in Chapter 4, there are key fundamentals to this journey, and "the district having a management process that focuses on accountability for results expected from the plan" should be considered as you move forward.

With the district strategic plan in place our first thought was to share it with the principals, step back, and watch the joy they would express at the opportunity to create an aligned school improvement plan. Oh . . . if it were only that simple! As Fullan detailed in *Turnaround Leadership* (2006) when he provided the example of the York Region School District, there are five basic components in this successful reform effort and three of them must be considered at this point—numbers one, two, and four:

1. Clearly articulated vision and commitment of success for all children

2. Systemwide plan and framework for continuous improvement

3. The use of data to drive instruction and identify resources

4. Capacity building at the principal and teacher level

5. Establishing professional learning communities at all levels

The board accomplished the first component with the district vision and mission and component two with the strategic plan and endorsement of the framework for continuous improvement as the expected approach. All lights were green and we were ready to go because we had more data than we knew what to do with. We took off, burning rubber all the way, and left the principals and teachers in a cloud of strategic planning confusion!

Component four should have given us a big yellow light but we paid it no heed and pushed forward by bringing principals and their leadership teams in for two mind-numbing days of strategic planning training without ever developing their capacity to understand the purpose and urgency of the work. After all, it was only about creating a plan, and we were giving them a template to fill in—how hard could it be?

Principal and leadership team capacity to do this work was a big red light that we didn't see coming. Ordinarily, principals and teachers are not trained in strategic planning. They are not born knowing how to analyze data, create goals, define strategies, and develop deployment plans. They need training, modeling, practice, feedback, and coaching in order to understand how to create a strategic plan, and support in deploying it. We were so busy burning rubber at the green light of the board strategic plan that we neglected to develop the capacity of our school leadership teams to execute the next level of aligned planning at the school level.

When developing the capacity of employees to perform the defined work to high levels, you must create a system of support. It is easy to provide a few hours of strategic planning training and send them away to do their work, as long as you don't expect great plans and you absolutely don't expect them to deploy the plans. If you expect great plans and the deployment of those plans, you have to implement a systematic approach to building the capacity of the school leadership teams to do the work.

We developed the school improvement planning template, designed to ensure that a plan–do–study–act approach to strategic planning was followed (see Figure 3.1, page 22). Hands-on facilitated experience with the template was provided, and schools used their own data to determine their gaps and follow the template to create their plan. This work was completed over two days with the training divided into the components of the template. Once the gaps were identified through data analysis, teams were taught how to create SMART (specific, measureable, aligned, results driven, time bound) three-year overall goals. Facilitators provided feedback to the teams, and revisions were made on the goals based on their learning. When the teams had identified key gaps and developed one well-written three-year goal, they were then coached on creating a one-year, aligned target goal. Feedback was provided that increased their learning and ensured solid goal development. The training continued through identification of an approach to achieve the target goal, creating a deployment plan for the approach, and defining resources and professional development that would be needed to implement the plan. By the end of day two, all teams had developed a school improvement plan for one gap area and developed a plan for how they were going to share this plan with their staff, train them on the SIP template, receive feedback on the first goal, and create buy-in for their work. The overall SMART goal, target goal, and approach or strategy from Central Elementary is shown in the sidebar.

The *school improvement plan* (SIP) training/coaching approach was the beginning of building the capacity of leadership teams to develop their strategic plans aligned to the district priorities. To avoid the earlier mistake of "drive-by" professional development on strategic planning, we created a support process to continue the coaching of leadership teams in each cycle. In this process, first-cycle SIPs are sent to the chief quality officer for review and feedback. Feedback is provided to SIP leadership teams electronically (see Figure 3.2, page 28 for an example) and teams revise plans based on the feedback. Deployment occurs over a nine-week period and, at the end of the cycle, SIP leadership teams receive one hour of face-to-face coaching based on a SWOT (strengths, weaknesses, opportunities for improvement, and threats) analysis of the implementation of their SIP. This coaching session identifies opportunities for improvement (OFIs)

Overall SMART Goal: By June 2012, 96% of the students in grades K–5 will be at or above grade level in math as determined by Predictive Assessments and EOG data.

Aligned, One-Year SMART Target Goal: By June 2009, the students will increase math proficiency from 85.5% to 87.3% in grades 3–5 as measured by Common Formative Assessments, Predictive Assessments, and End-of-Grade Test data. Students in grades K–2 will increase math proficiency from 92.8% to 95.2% as measured by Common Formative Assessments and Predictive Assessments.

Strategy or Approach for the First Quarter: Weekly math interventions will be provided for identified at-risk students who are scoring below proficient on Predictive Assessments. The interventions will be based on identified math gaps and will be in addition to their regular math instruction.

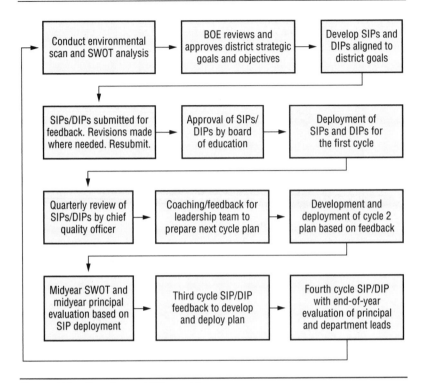

Figure 5.1 Flowchart of SIP coaching process.

and next steps, which are rolled into the next cycle's deployment plan. This PDSA coaching process of the SIP is designed to develop the capacity of the leadership teams in each school. Figure 5.1 details the SIP coaching process used for school leadership team development.

Once the school leadership team coaching process was in place we developed and implemented a similar process for district department teams to support division/department improvement plans.

LESSONS LEARNED

1. A well-trained board that communicates clear direction is the beginning, not the end. Once the district has a clearly defined direction, you must be cautious about speeding forward. Take the time to put a plan in place to support school and district department teams in developing the capacity to create strong department and school plans or the priorities of the district will not be accomplished.

2. Defining a group of people as a leadership team or a goal team does not make them a team. Who knew??

The next red light that brought us to a screeching halt was the inability of our school and department teams to work well together to deploy the new plans. Teams need training and coaching on how to become high-performing teams. By not recognizing this deficit, the deployment of our well-written, well-coached plans stopped at another red light. Building strong teams became an essential addition to the professional development offered to our leadership and goal teams. Fullan has as Secret Two in *Six Secrets of Change* (2008), "Connect Peers with Purpose." He states, the "peer interaction must be purposeful and must be characterized by high-capacity knowledge and skills. Leaders have to provide direction, create the conditions for effective peer interaction, and intervene along the way when things are not working as well as they could." The group approach that we took to strategic planning was right on target, but we failed to assist our groups in understanding how to work as high-performing teams. Fullan (2008) further explains that "knowledge flows as people pursue and continuously learn what works best," and our approach of collaborative planning teams focused on best practices to close gaps through the strategic planning process provided the environment for this flow of knowledge.

We developed and implemented professional development aimed at the core basic structures our school leadership teams and goal teams would need to have to work collaboratively. This skill development coupled with our PDSA approach to strategic planning has enabled our leadership and goal teams to move forward in the development and implementation of good strategic plans designed to close gaps and support the district priorities.

In order to build a strong team structure, we trained and coached the collaborative leadership and goal teams in seven key areas:

- Collaboratively create a team mission that clarifies the common purpose of the team.

- Develop and implement an effective and efficient process to communicate within and externally to other teams and school partners.

- Identify group norms that will provide focus for the team work time.

- Assign appropriate roles that will enable the team to function effectively and efficiently.

- Define and adopt processes that will assist the team in conducting effective meetings (that is, agenda format, minutes template, and so on).

- Define the empowerment structure that will enable the team to make data-driven decisions to raise achievement and close gaps through the SIP process.

- Implement a consistent process to evaluate team meetings and improve team performance.

CONNECTING TO RESEARCH

Kotter, in his book *Leading Change* (1996), talks about the barriers to empowerment and determines that while employees often understand the vision and will work to make it a reality, they are sometimes unable to move forward with the work due to several barriers, one of which is lacking the skills needed to do the work. We discovered that once we were able to develop the skills of our school teams in the area of strategic planning and operating as a team, the quality of our plans increased exponentially.

Fullan (2008), as discussed earlier, supports this notion, and the research he has completed on organizations that have experienced significant improvement defines having a clear purpose that is understood and embraced by the group as key to success. As Jim Collins shared in *Good to Great* (2001), "Good-to-great management teams consist of people who debate vigorously in search of the best answers, yet who unify behind decisions, regardless of parochial interests."

Our decision to focus on a systematic process to assist schools and departments in creating strategic plans aligned to the district priorities and to develop teams to deploy those plans is on target.

A FOCUS ON RESULTS

While it is important to have the board of education understand and endorse the district priorities, it must be recognized that it is just the beginning of strategic planning. The final result must be aligned plans at all levels of the organization that will support those priorities and be focused on closing key gaps in performance. Once we realized we couldn't just move forward with a green light when the board approved our direction, we began focusing on developing the capacity of our employees to create strategic plans and track the performance of our teams with deployment of their plans. Feedback was based on high performance in key areas of planning and results at the end of each cycle of implementation. The quality of school and department improvement plans increased with each cycle, and the work of each level of the organization is now driven by those plans and not by the "Wow, I hope this works!" approach.

Figure 5.2 is representative of the progress we have made in identified areas that are critical to the development of a strategic plan that, when implemented, will produce results. When a strategic plan has a clear goal but does not have a clearly defined strategy or approach to reach that goal, the results will not improve. The same is true when the approach is clearly defined but the deployment plan does not ensure that deployment with fidelity occurs and there is no measure to determine how well deployment is occurring. This error report reflects the progress made in critical areas of the development of key parts of the plan.

We have found that fidelity of implementation of the approach to reach the goal is the most critical part of the plan. Research-based best-practice approaches are only as good as the fidelity of implementation of the approach. Figure 5.3 is a visual representation of the challenge we have

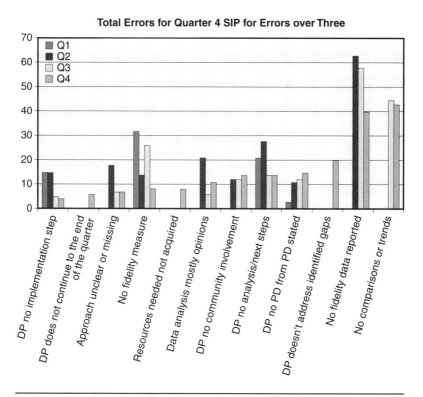

Figure 5.2   School improvement plan error report.

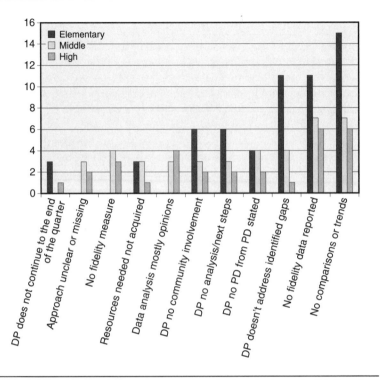

Figure 5.3 Number of schools, by level, with identified gaps in fidelity of implementation of SIP process.

faced in measuring and improving fidelity of implementation of key strategic approaches.

As we have increased the capacity of leadership teams at the school and district department level to create and implement better strategic plans, we have seen academic and operational improvement in such areas as academic achievement, reduction of bus driver overtime, supplemental sales in child nutrition, workers' compensation loss ratio, and reduction of bus discipline referrals. Figures 5.4 through 5.8 demonstrate the increased performance levels in these areas.

Strategic planning is key to alignment and direction. Fidelity of implementation of the plan insures both high performance and continuous improvement in our schools and departments. The results speak for themselves.

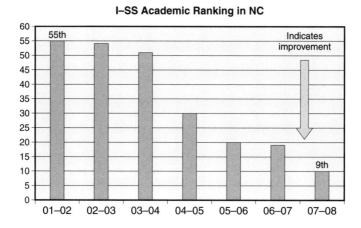

Figure 5.4 Composite ranking of Iredell–Statesville School District in the state of North Carolina.

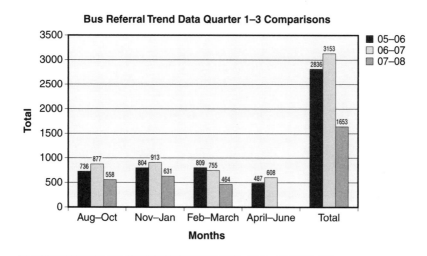

Figure 5.5 Bus discipline referrals over three quarters.

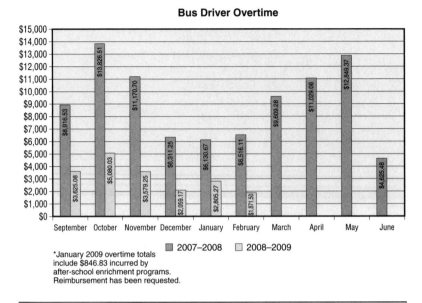

Figure 5.6 Bus driver overtime reduction.

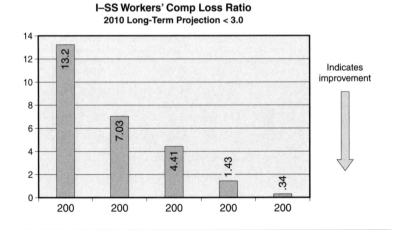

Figure 5.7 Workers' compensation loss ratio.

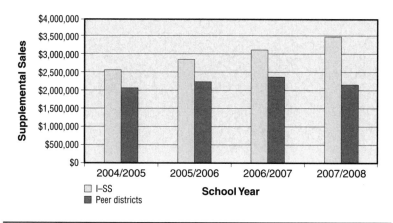

Figure 5.8   Supplemental sales in child nutrition program.

6

Red Light #6—
Teacher Resistance:
The Longest Light

by Terry Holliday

THE STORY

Over the past few years, we have had many opportunities to speak to audiences from California to Maine to Sweden. During the question and answer sessions that follow, one question is always asked by a member of the audience: "How do you get people to actually change the classroom or school culture?" This question underscores the fact that the principal or superintendent asking the question has tried to implement a change in school or classroom structures in the past and has met with significant resistance to the change initiative. What these principals and district leaders have discovered is the longest red light in education change. We have all sat at those long red lights and watched every other traveler moving before we get to move. Every locality seems to have at least one long red light that should be nominated for the "longest red light in the nation" award. When I talk to superintendents and principals, they often brag about or bemoan the fact that the quality reform effort will not work in their school or district because of the entrenchment and/or distrust of teachers. The red light of classroom teacher resistance and distrust is real and it is a long one. It takes a great deal of patience and understanding to overcome this obstacle. Leaders will take many detours and turn right on red at many points in the journey to find a solution to teacher resistance.

We can hardly blame teachers for resistance to change initiatives. If you have been in education for at least 10 to 20 years, you have probably seen a wave of reform. From the science reform spawned by Sputnik to the more recent No Child Left Behind, the graveyards of failed reform efforts serve as monuments to good intentions that have produced little or no beneficial change. The comments of educators when introduced to change efforts are usually the same—"we tried this before and it did not work," "I was here before this superintendent and I will be here after he is gone," "I listen and

63

nod in agreement when in workshops and then go back and close my classroom door and do what I have always done," "if those people would just get in the real world of my classroom they would know that this stuff does not work," and "they will never give us the money and resources we need to implement this stuff, so I am not even going to bother trying."

One of the major tenets of the quality reform initiative is to reduce variation in processes and improve overall quality of results. What this means in education is to reduce the major variations in classrooms and improve the overall results of student learning. Teachers often see this as a challenge to innovation, creativity, and autonomy. Teachers will describe a quality initiative as trying to make every teacher teach the same thing in the same way at the same time. Of course, that is completely opposite from what a learning model promotes; however, it is extremely difficult for leaders to communicate the actual intent of a learning model because some of the first steps in a learning model are to establish standards, common goals for learning, common assessments for learning, and common interventions for groups of students.

In our work over the last 12 years, we have discovered a model that has proven to be successful in addressing teacher concerns over the reduction in variation among classrooms and ensuring that teachers are at least deploying components of the model. The overall model is our *raising achievement and closing gaps* model (see Figure 4.1, page 33); however, the core of the model is the *instructional facilitator*. Let me back up a little. We did not start with the model and we did not start with the title of "instructional facilitator"—that came later. The instructional facilitator component has been 12 long years in the making, and we have run up against many red lights in our journey to implement the model. The roles and responsibilities of an instructional facilitator can be found in Appendix B.

The instructional facilitator model started in a small western North Carolina school system in the Blue Ridge Mountains. When we started training school leaders in the quality reform initiative, we knew that to really make a difference in learning results we had to get the reform to the classroom. Our first big mistake was in training. We thought that we could identify a classroom teacher in each building and give them "training in a box" components of quality. So, we tried the "train the trainer" model by training the classroom representatives in systems thinking, then giving them the "box components" and asking the trainers to train classroom teachers in seven modules during after-school training throughout the year. Of course, our trainers also had to continue with their normal classroom assignments! What we discovered was that we were offering random acts of improvement in training. We did not require any follow-up to training activities, the training was mainly theoretically based, and there was little or no coaching and support for deploying the training modules. So we had run a red light and had basically created resistance to the quality reform model before we had even started actually asking teachers to do something different in their classrooms.

Our next step in the journey toward instructional facilitators came in an elementary Title I school. One of our principals had been involved with an instructional coach model in another school system and wanted to try a similar approach at her school. We thought this would be a great way to try and implement some of the quality reform components in a Title I school, and of course the Title I regulations helped us implement the effort. The model was called *Title I coordinator*. The coordinator worked with teacher assistants who had been hired for pullout components of the Title I program. Students were pulled out of classrooms for small group instruction on learning objectives that they had been unsuccessful with in the classroom. Prior to the coordinator model, the students had been pulled out of the classroom and the teacher assistants had worked with the students. However, there had been little or no communication between the classroom teacher and the teacher assistant. The teacher assistants had very little training and they were basically using test preparation materials that had been aligned with the North Carolina standard course of study. In other words, the students were working on additional worksheets and there was no guarantee that the students were working on the learning objectives with which they were struggling.

In most cases, the students were getting extra reading help or basic math skills worksheets. The coordinator started by closing the communication gap between the classroom teacher and the teacher assistant. The coordinator then started training the teacher assistants on instructional strategies that were best suited for individual students who were struggling. The model changed from "pull out" to "push in," and the coordinator implemented methods that tracked the students' progress, moved the hoarded resources from the media center and Title I resource center to classrooms where they could be used every day, provided customer feedback from classroom teachers to the Title I program, developed a mission and goals for the Title I program, and informed the classroom teacher of which strategies seemed to work best for which students. It was not long before classroom teachers actually started asking for training on some of the interventions since they saw that students were actually making progress. Also, by doing a push-in model, we learned that classroom teachers were not consistently deploying the North Carolina standard course of study. As district leaders in this reform effort, we finally saw that job-embedded coaching and support, common curriculum standards, improved communication, and monitoring student progress tied to the reform efforts were the strategies that might help us overcome teacher resistance. Of course, we probably could have just asked teachers what they needed and gotten the same answer without the trials and errors we had committed over a three-year period of top-down initiatives. Prior to leaving this school system, we had gone from a Title I coordinator to a lead teacher model deployed in most elementary schools; however, we were not very successful in getting the model deployed in middle or high schools. Who would have guessed that secondary teachers are even more resistant to change than elementary teachers?

When we moved to Iredell–Statesville, we had learned from our mistakes and, as described in earlier chapters, we started the quality reform initiative by modeling the change we expected and developing strong relationships in the schools and the community. We started the lead teacher model in our Title I schools. Almost two-thirds of our elementary schools were Title I schools, however, and with No Child Left Behind (NCLB) requirements being our support we implemented the lead teacher model in our lowest-performing elementary schools. We had three lead teachers and three assistant principals/lead teachers deployed in six elementary schools. The interview process involved district-level and school-level administrators. Since Title I was funding the position, the district had a great deal of control over the job duties and responsibilities of the position. We have learned through the years that a very clear job description and accountability for responsibilities are essential. The ultimate control of the position must remain with the district; however, the principal plays a key role in the support and success of the position (see reference in Appendix B, specifically items 1–4 and 12).

Our first year of deployment of the lead teacher model in Iredell–Statesville featured a lot of stand-up training on the theoretical basis for a classroom/school model based on the Baldrige Criteria. About midway through the year, we learned that we needed to change to a more practical and classroom-based approach. The lead teachers began working with grade-level teams, provided small bits of training, and then assigned homework for the classroom teachers. We learned that teachers must deploy, and they can only deploy small bits at a time. We also learned that unless the district had some accountability for fidelity of deployment of training, we would continue to have mixed results based on "random acts of improvement."

In our second year of deployment we tried to eliminate some silos at the district level. We turned our gifted teacher coaches and some of our exceptional children (EC) coaches into lead teachers. We were fairly certain by this time that the lead teacher had to be a job-embedded coach. The lead teacher had to attend grade-level meetings—which at the time we were calling *communities of practice*. The lead teacher was at the school to provide coaching, training, resources, and support. The lead teacher was the district's intervention for low-performing schools and any elementary school that had a subgroup not meeting NCLB standards. The learning we gained during this time was that just placing people in the position of lead teacher did not assure they would be successful. As Jim Collins said in *Good to Great* (2001), "we needed to get the right people in the right seat on the bus." This meant that we needed a systemic and systematic process for selecting, training, and retaining lead teachers.

By the third year of our deployment, Title II had changed focus from lowering class size to improving the quality of teachers and instruction. This change allowed I–SS to implement the lead teacher model in all of our elementary schools. North Carolina had also started providing more funding for at-risk schools at the middle and high school levels, so we were able to access this funding to place a few lead teachers at the middle and high school levels. By this time, we became more and more convinced that curriculum mapping, quality tools training, and a focus on fidelity of deployment of our model for raising achievement and closing gaps were essential components of success.

By the fourth year, our model for raising achievement and closing gaps had been well defined, and in the schools where the model was deployed with support of a lead teacher and deployed with fidelity we were beginning to see significant changes in student learning results. It was during this year that we developed a systemic approach to the recruitment and training of lead teachers. The standards for a lead teacher were: successful deployment of our continuous improvement classroom model, minimum of five years teaching, and commitment to a yearlong training pool. The level of quality of the applicants and the quality of work of lead teachers has increased significantly since implementing this systemic approach.

Over the last three years, we have changed the title of *lead teacher* to *instructional facilitator.* We would prefer *instructional coach;* however, state funding requirements have driven the need for the title. During these three years, we have learned that instructional facilitators need to meet often (almost weekly) as a team to coach and support each other. During this professional development time, they prepare for the training, coaching, and support of classroom teachers. The key driver for the instructional facilitators is the *professional learning community* (PLC) *team work requirements* that I–SS developed (see Appendix B, specifically items 1, 2, 7, and 9). These requirements are the accountability piece of the model. They drive the work of PLCs and ensure that the work is done with fidelity. Also, built within the PLC matrix are the district-required professional development components. During the 2006–07 school year we began to implement the classroom walk-through model. What we discovered was that teachers were not utilizing high-yield instructional strategies. Through the instructional facilitator model we began deploying training for two high-yield strategies per year, and the classroom walk-through data reveal whether teachers are actually deploying the strategies. Also, through the instructional facilitator model we deploy our training for continuous classroom improvement. This model requires the use of a plan–do–study–act cycle (see examples in Appendix C) in every classroom that eventually trains students on how to utilize PDSA in their student data notebooks and student-led parent conferences. The instructional facilitators meet weekly with PLCs at the elementary and middle school levels, and at the high school level they meet weekly with PLC chairs and train them on the I–SS expectations. High school principals and assistant principals are also trained to assist with helping PLCs meet I–SS expectations. During the last two years, we have discovered a great need for training, coaching, and support in the development of learning standards in kid-friendly language, common formative assessments, analysis of classroom data, second-level intervention strategies, and differentiation. Our instructional facilitator model provides the job-embedded coaching, training, support, and resources for all of these needs.

CONNECTING TO RESEARCH: INTERNATIONAL REPORT AND IMPLICATIONS FOR I–SS

One of the research components that helped validate our work in I–SS is an international report completed by the McKinsey Consulting Company that studied 25 school systems in the world. The report specifically looked at the top ten performing school systems in the world as measured by international assessments.

The report concluded that simply providing more funding for education will not necessarily impact student learning outcomes. The United States is an excellent example of this finding. From 1980 to 2005, spending on education increased by 73 percent while scores on national and international assessments of literacy and numeracy remained relatively flat.

Another finding was that decreases in class size do not lead to improvements in student learning outcomes. In North Carolina, this has been the banner initiative for over eight years and has produced limited results. As a matter of fact, I–SS recently removed class size measures as a strategic goal. The McKinsey report documented 112 international studies of which only nine studies revealed any significant correlation between decreased class size and improved student learning outcomes—and these were minor improvements in student learning outcomes. One hundred three of the studies showed no correlation or a negative correlation between decreased class size and student learning outcomes.

What the McKinsey report did reveal as having a huge impact on student learning is the quality of the classroom teacher. The McKinsey report revealed that high-performing school systems around the world have three things in common:

1. Getting the right people to become teachers

2. Developing them into effective instructors

3. Ensuring that the system is able to deliver the best possible instruction to *every* child

These findings validate what we have done in I–SS. We have greatly enhanced our recruitment efforts and our partnerships with universities so that we are recruiting only highly qualified teachers. We have improved our screening and interview processes so that we hire the best candidates. However, simply obtaining highly qualified teachers does not ensure that they are effective instructors.

The McKinsey report recommended three approaches to improving instruction: provide coaches, instructional leadership, and opportunities for teachers to learn from each other. We do all three in I–SS. We 1) *provide coaches* (instructional facilitators and literacy coaches) to help all teachers improve the quality of instruction. We work with every principal to ensure they are spending the majority of their time on 2) *instructional leadership.* Finally, we provide a structure called professional learning communities so that 3) *teachers can learn from each other.* We do not spend money on sending teachers to state and national conferences unless they are presenting and enhancing the reputation of the school system. The findings from the research and the McKinsey report are very clear. Improving instructional skills and the quality of teaching is done through application and on-the-job coaching and modeling.

The final strategy for improving the quality of teachers and instruction is to monitor the expectation that every child can and will learn to high levels. In I–SS, we are often criticized for monitoring what we expect through quality assurance processes. However, the findings are very clear on this issue: if you do not inspect what you expect, you will not get improvement. It is important to our school system to decrease the variability of instruction while not negatively impacting innovation.

Equity of instruction and equity of student learning outcomes is possible. Quite often, citizens and even educators will say that poor children and children of color can not learn at high levels. Local, state, national, and international results should have long put this belief to rest. Schools can and have compensated for the disadvantages resulting from a student's home environment. To believe anything else would question the basic need for schools and education (see Figures 6.7 and 6.8).

Another key research source for the I–SS model has been the work of Doug Reeves. In his most recent work, *Reframing Teacher Leadership* (2008), we found the key issue. In order to refocus the classroom from being a teacher-centered classroom to being a learning-centered classroom, the teacher and administrator relationship must transcend traditional relationships. In I–SS that looks like principals developing their instructional observation skills by being paired with instructional facilitators for the development of inter-rater reliability on our classroom walk-through model. It looks like principals attending PLCs and reviewing classroom walk-through data in a nonthreatening and nonevaluative atmosphere. It involves principals talking to teachers about what resources, training, coaching, and support are needed to improve instruction. It looks like principals meeting with instructional facilitators each month and receiving training, coaching, and support on high-yield instructional strategies and classroom action research models embedded within our plan–do–study–act model. It looks like principals attending training and then working with teachers to develop the wording of kid-friendly learning standards. It looks like principals sitting down with teachers in PLCs and reviewing grade-level learning goals and student performance on common formative assessments to identify the strengths and weaknesses of students, classes, and the school.

Reeves enumerates several key components required for reframing teacher leadership. One of these is direct observation and feedback from teacher to teacher. Our instructional facilitators are *never* placed in an evaluative role. They become teacher leaders and they have responsibility to not only observe teachers but also to provide modeling and observation opportunities for classroom teachers. The tools used to ensure feedback are the classroom walk-through discussion in PLCs and direct feedback from the instructional facilitator on the classroom teacher's deployment of our classroom continuous improvement model, which includes plan–do–study–act cycles, student data notebooks, best practice instructional strategy boards, and best practice sharing between PLCs and schools.

Reeves also recommends a basic component of action research. In I–SS, action research is documented through our plan–do–study–act model (see PDSA models in Appendix C).

In I–SS, classrooms answer the question "What do students need to learn?" by placing the short-term (usually weekly) learning objective in the *plan* part of the template. The learning objective must be tied to the North

Carolina standard course of study and be worded in kid-friendly language. The classroom discussion then centers on the *do* part of the template. What will the teacher do and what will the student do to help meet the learning objective? This is where the teacher may rely on research-proven instructional strategies or best practice strategies shared by the members of his/ her PLC. Students use strategies that they have gained over the years that fit their learning style. During the *study* phase of the cycle, measurement takes place to determine if the students met the learning goal for the learning cycle. The students and teacher analyze what worked and what did not work in the learning cycle. This action research cycle has led teachers to discover many excellent instructional strategies that they had never used before, and the cycle also allows students to become more responsible for their own learning in that they learn what strategies work for them to be successful in reaching the learning goals. The action research then transcends to organizational learning through the district instructional facilitator meeting where validated and reliable instructional strategies are shared with other schools and grade levels. Many if not most best practices are then documented on our Web page for future teachers and future classrooms to utilize.

Reeves also discusses the necessity of job-embedded professional development. Our instructional facilitator model and our PLC model provide this job-embedded professional development. Given the challenges of budgets and cost of travel to conferences, the concept of job-embedded professional development is not only a best practice, it is now an essential. Finally, Reeves talks about the fidelity of deployment of any instructional strategy or intervention. In the research documented by Reeves, the payoff on a strategy or intervention does not really happen until an organization reaches about 90 percent deployment with fidelity. In the results section of this chapter, we will provide two examples that verify this research finding.

In this book we have often talked about methods to overcome resistance. Reeves asks in his book, "In spite of mountains of evidence, why are teachers resistant to action research?" He lists the following as the top reasons provided by teachers, and throughout this book we have documented all of these reasons through the questions and responses we have gotten from teachers:

- Time
- Union won't let us
- Board won't let us
- Administrators won't support us

- Culture resists change

- Staff won't let us

- It won't work here

- This too shall pass

Two of my favorite authors are Doug Reeves and Robert Marzano. In his research for *What Works in Schools* (2003), Marzano describes the impact of schools and quality of teaching on student learning results. Table 6.1 represents what happens to children who enter third grade scoring at the 50th percentile and the impact of the school and classroom teacher on student results at the end of fifth grade.

Reeves also provided commentary on the impact of the classroom teacher on student learning. Reeves first discusses the *Pygmalion effect:*

- If we expect our actions to have impact on student learning,
  then we will impact student learning.

- If we do not think our actions can overcome the impact of student
  demographics on learning, then we will not impact student
  learning.

For those who believe student achievement is most influenced by demographics, schools and classrooms have a 6.14 percent gain on average. For those who believe student achievement is most influenced by faculty actions and instructional strategies, there is an 18.4 percent gain on average. Actions that reflect beliefs show almost triple the gain in student achievement. The McKinsey report had similar findings. Student learning results improvements are more directly related to the quality of instruction than class size, demographics, and expenditures per pupil.

Table 6.1   Impacts of teacher and school on student achievement.

School and teacher scenario	Achievement percentile after two years
Average school and average teacher	50th
Least effective school and least effective teacher	3rd
Most effective school and least effective teacher	37th
Least effective school and most effective teacher	63rd
Most effective school and average teacher	78th
Most effective school and most effective teacher	96th

A FOCUS ON RESULTS

The question for readers then becomes, do the results in I–SS document the strategies listed and the connections made to the research? You be the judge.

I–SS has moved from being below state average among North Carolina school systems on composite ranking for end-of-grade and end-of-course tests to being among the top ten in North Carolina (see Figure 6.1) while maintaining expenditures among the lowest 10 school systems in the state ($700 per pupil below state average).

We discovered what Doug Reeves meant about fidelity of deployment. Figure 6.2 shows what happened in classrooms where our exceptional children (EC) reading intervention model was deployed with 90 percent to 100 percent fidelity (96 percent of students achieved at grade level). Where the model was not deployed with fidelity, we had major reductions in percentage of students meeting grade-level requirements on end-of-grade testing.

We also discovered the fidelity of deployment with our model of continuous classroom improvement. In Table 6.2, we find that teachers who deployed with fidelity at or above 90 percent had significantly (all correlations above .75) higher scale score gain on state assessments than teachers who deployed with low fidelity.

Implementation of the I–SS model for raising achievement and closing gaps led to significant increases in student achievement. In Figure 6.3 the reading scores for grades 3–8 are reported. Reading achievement improved

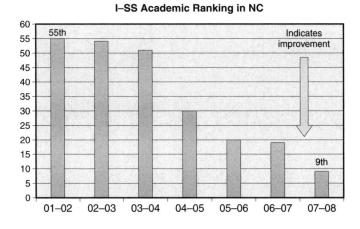

Figure 6.1 Overall academic ranking in North Carolina.

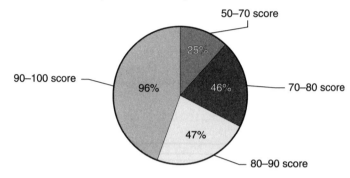

**EC Reading Percent Proficient in
Comparison to Fidelity Scores 2006–2007**

50–70 score

90–100 score

96%

25%

46%

70–80 score

47%

80–90 score

Figure 6.2 Exceptional children (EC) performance in corrective reading
classrooms.

Table 6.2 Impact of I–SS continuous improvement model
on scale score gains.

Subject	High deployment	Low deployment
Reading 3–5	11.05	–4.11
Math 3–5	10.57	7.42
Reading 6–8	–.98	–3.39
Math 6–8	3.64	3.36

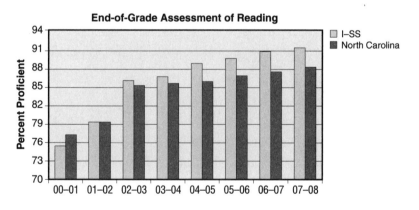

End-of-Grade Assessment of Reading

I–SS
North Carolina

Percent Proficient

00–01 01–02 02–03 03–04 04–05 05–06 06–07 07–08

Figure 6.3 Longitudinal performance for I–SS on North Carolina reading
assessment.

from a ranking of 75th among the 115 North Carolina school systems to 20th. Actual percentage of students scoring proficient on the reading assessment improved from 75 percent to over 90 percent. At the same time overall achievement was being improved, two very important achievement gaps were being closed. In Figure 6.4 the achievement for the African-American subgroup is reported. The achievement gap was closed from a 23-point gap to a 12-point gap. The I–SS gap was higher than the state achievement gap in 2002, but by 2008 the achievement gap was significantly below the state average achievement gap. Similar results are reported in Figure 6.5

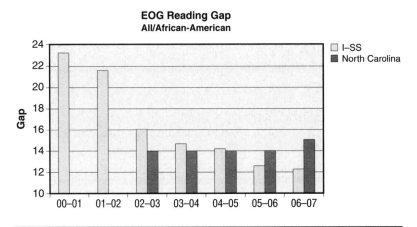

Figure 6.4   I–SS closing the achievement gap for African-American students.

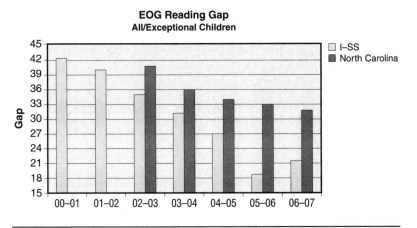

Figure 6.5   I–SS closing the achievement gap for exceptional children.

for children with exceptional needs. The reading gap for exceptional children improved from a 42-point gap to a 21-point gap, which is significantly below the state gap of 32 points.

Other important areas of comparison are high school graduation rates and SAT scores. In Figure 6.6, the No Child Left Behind cohort graduation rate is reported. I–SS moved from being in the lowest ten school districts in North Carolina for graduation rates to a rank of 11th among the 115 school systems for the class of 2008. The graduation rate improved from 58.5 percent to 80.7 percent. Also, the SAT scores reported in Figure 6.7 show a five-year trend of improvement from a combined verbal and math score of 991 to 1056. This 65-point overall improvement moved I–SS from a rank of 57th in North Carolina to a rank of seventh among 115 school systems.

In summary, the challenge for leaders is to reduce variability in classrooms for the most important result of all—student learning. The challenge in reducing variability is in not having a negative impact on teacher creativity and innovation. In I–SS, we do have common standards, common assessments, common goals, common time for meeting and planning, and high expectations for all students. However, we feel that the plan–do–study–act cycle provides the template for action research. Through action research, we feel that teachers have the ultimate ability to identify what works in classrooms for all types of students and all types of learning objectives. What we do not think teachers should have is the autonomy to implement bad practice on unsuspecting children. Many teachers have worked

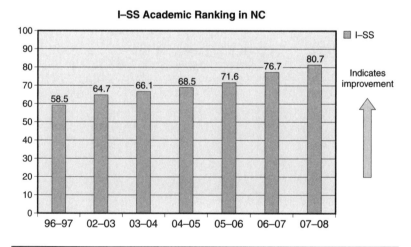

Figure 6.6   Longitudinal results for cohort graduation rate.

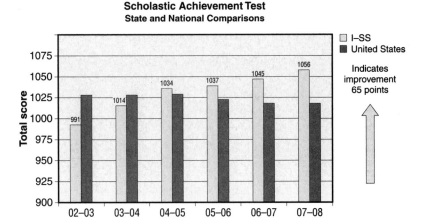

Figure 6.7 I–SS results for Scholastic Achievement Test.

behind closed doors for years, and they will eventually be your loudest critics of this type of reform initiative. The data will reveal the areas where student growth and student learning are not happening. Then these critics will become very vocal, and they have the capability of undermining the reform work. The first five chapters of this book will help prepare you for this assured response and provide methods to overcome the challenge and move forward with this important work.

7

What's Next

by Terry Holliday

"**N**ow that you have received the Baldrige Award, what's next?" This is a routine inquiry following our presentations or in casual conversation with peers. The response is always the same—it was never really about the recognition, it was about the journey. I recently saw a quote on a Web site (despair.com): "The race for quality has no finish line—so technically, it's more like a death march." While the quote is humorous, we often feel like we *are* on a death march. No matter how high performing the school system, you will always have critics and cynics. The critics and cynics are often very vocal, and their attacks are frequently personal because they rarely have a logical and fact-based point of view. It's just too hard to argue with the data!

What's next for I–SS is more of the same with a more concentrated effort. Several focus areas have emerged over the past few years, and this chapter will document our continued efforts in these areas—benchmarks, benchmarking, value-added SAS, and process management of a cross-functional organization.

BENCHMARKS

Our work in this area has been going on for a few years. Our efforts were enhanced by two key partnerships. The first partnership was with David Bayless, a retired professor, researcher, and statistician. His work with North Carolina State University and eventually Westat, Inc. focused on numerous large-scale assessment projects and business projects. David was part of the development team for *The Team Handbook for Educators* (1994) and has conducted a great deal of research in process variation and control. Our work with David and his wife Nancy has been spread over 10 years in two different school systems. We started with an internal benchmark process that attempted to identify teachers and schools who were producing results that could be identified as breakthrough performance. This work has spread over the last few years to an analysis of all the schools and school systems in North Carolina. David has developed a *process variation control and analysis methodology* (PVCAM) that analyzes performance of processes at the state, district, school, grade, and curriculum level. While a separate book would be needed to explain the process and the analysis software, what Dave and Nancy have done is to place all school districts, schools, grade levels, and curricula on control charts to determine those processes that are creating continuous improvement and those processes that are creating breakthrough improvement. In recent years, Dave and Nancy have created correlation charts that combine with control charts. The correlation charts have been very valuable as we move toward benchmarking. The correlation charts relate district and school performance on state assessments, showing the percentage of students with disabilities and those who are economically disadvantaged. The charts show those districts and schools that are performing significantly above districts with similar percentages of students with disabilities and economically disadvantaged students. Once the districts and schools are identified as being high-performing systems, then the benchmarking process can begin with identification of best practices and instructional strategies being used.

The other partnership that has grown over the past few years has been with APQC in Houston, Texas. We first started working with APQC during their benchmark study of professional development practices in school systems. APQC has long worked with business leaders throughout the world to document key processes in organizations and to benchmark the results from key steps in processes, and key processes themselves. Thanks to the patriotic spirit of founder Jack Grayson, APQC turned its attention to United States educational systems a few years ago and developed a model for school system processes. He then turned his attention to gathering data on key steps and processes for benchmark purposes. Our first involvement was in the gathering of benchmark data for professional development. Through our introduction, we soon realized that our Baldrige and continuous improvement focus had helped us create professional development processes and results that were among the highest performers in the study. That finding led us to become one of the best-practice sites for the next benchmark study, which was data-driven decision making.

BENCHMARKING

While the benchmark process allows organizations to compare themselves against the performance of relevant comparable and top-performing organizations, the next step is benchmarking. Benchmarking requires action to learn what the benchmark organizations do to produce the results they are getting from processes. Once best practices are identified, then organizations are responsible for knowledge sharing at the organization and personal level. Knowledge transfer becomes critical as organizations have internal changes in leadership of key processes.

With the Bayless PVCAM process our principals were able to identify both internal and external schools and grade levels that were performing at a significantly higher level than their school or grade level was performing. As a reminder, the benchmarks were with schools that had similar percentages of students with disabilities and percentages of economically disadvantaged students. So we were comparing *apples* to *apples!* The principals established a systemic process for contacting the schools through the principal and then implemented an interview process that captured best practices. The principals then met by grade level and shared what they had learned. The principals discovered that in many cases the benchmark schools were utilizing similar approaches; however, they were deploying the approaches with fidelity and had actually limited the number of approaches to improving instruction in their schools.

With the APQC benchmarking process, there was a very systematic interview process for gathering the necessary comparative data from process steps and process results. At the end of the data-gathering period, all school systems involved in the benchmark study gathered together to review the findings from the study. There have been many powerful sessions where best-practice knowledge was shared and transferred. School systems who were not involved in the study can access the results of the benchmark study and the best practices learned from the benchmarking sessions by contacting APQC.

PROCESS MANAGEMENT IN A CROSS-FUNCTIONAL ORGANIZATION

For years, education focused on an input model for improvement. The old accreditation models focused on the number of books in the library, curricula developed, number of teachers with master's degrees, pay levels of teachers and administrators, and the number of continuing education units received annually. With the advent of No Child Left Behind, the focus moved from inputs to accountability for results. Schools, school systems, and students are now judged as to whether they are a failure or not by a one-time assessment that is not common across the nation and not based on common standards. What is an acceptable standard in one state may not even be passing in another state. A process management model merges the two models of inputs and outputs with the middle component of process management. Business has long referred to this model as an SIPOC model. SIPOC refers to *supplier* to *input* to *process* to *output* to *customer,* with guides such as policy, regulations, and laws guiding the steps in the flow, and enablers such as equipment, human resources, and technology supporting the overall flow.

In life, school, and business, everything we do is a process. Going to meetings is a process. Conducting meetings is a process. Getting up in the morning is a process.

Business ran their organizations in a functional management method. In other words, business created silos of operation thinking these were the most effective and efficient ways to manage business processes. Business created silos called finance, human resources, marketing, facilities, planning, and information technology. Does this sound familiar to educators? However, what business learned throughout the last two decades is that processes are really cross-functional. Business found out the hard way that the functional silo method was creating suboptimization, turf wars, high costs, red tape, bureaucracy, waste, redundancy, errors, rework, and non-value-added steps in processes.

Over the years, we had heard much of this discussion during Baldrige training. We were sitting beside people from Cisco, Cargill, Motorola, AT&T, and numerous healthcare and small business employees who were driven by the bottom line to reduce waste and improve the effectiveness and efficiencies in their business or organization. Thanks to our partnership with APQC, we were able to attend a Michael Hammer workshop. This workshop focused on his book *Beyond Reengineering: How the Process-Centered Organization Will Change Our Work and Our Lives* (1996). This workshop was a leadership-changing event. We finally understood some of the reasons why we had resistance from our district-level leaders and why some of our silo department leads were not implementing the changes we needed.

From the Baldrige Criteria we find the following overall questions in the Process Management category (capitalized words are for emphasis by the Baldrige program):

- Describe HOW your organization designs its WORK SYSTEMS and determines its KEY PROCESSES to deliver student and STAKEHOLDER VALUE, maximize student LEARNING and success, prepare for potential emergencies, and achieve organizational success and SUSTAINABILITY.

- Describe HOW your organization designs, implements, manages, and improves its KEY WORK PROCESSES to deliver student and STAKEHOLDER VALUE and achieve organizational success and SUSTAINABILITY.

Many business, healthcare, nonprofit, government, and education organizations have benefited from the use of the Criteria to focus self-assessment and the development of a business model and framework for continuous improvement. What we learned from our interactions and studies with high-performing organizations was the universal focus on process management. After all, process management is where most of the work happens, and if processes are not effective and efficient, that is where most of the waste, redundancy, and non-value-added time occurs. Business found that a focus on process management led to the best results. Figure 7.1 was provided by Jack Grayson of APQC and is a composite of APQC's findings from working with international business leaders over several decades on the results when companies use process management.

APQC conducted eight benchmark studies of education, and their key findings were:

- Most educators do not *think* processes.

- They focus functionally, not *cross-functionally.*

- They do not *map* or *measure* processes.

- They do not *analyze* or *benchmark* processes.

- They don't *link* inputs—processes—outcomes

- They don't *manage* or *organize* by processes.

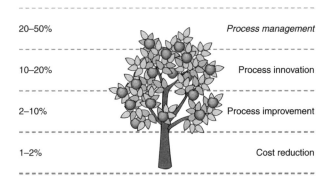

Figure 7.1 Business found large gains through a process focus.

- The ability to *improve performance* is very limited without improving processes.

When educators are asked why they do not change to a process-centered organization, these were some of the responses (see Figures 7.2 through 7.4):

- Focus is on functions, inputs, and outcomes
- Districts not accustomed to using data to compare themselves with others
- No common taxonomy of processes
- Low urgency to change
- No infrastructure for process management
- Don't know how to change

We found that I–SS was no different from other education organizations. In I–SS this focus on process management helped us to identify the source of a number of difficulties we had endured over our quality journey. While our finance officer supported our efforts, she did not understand why her department actually had to work on a department improvement plan. Our human resources and finance departments rarely talked with each other about teacher and position allocation and actually had dual and competing databases. Our quality department and curriculum department often engaged in turf wars over learning standards, school improvement plans, principal evaluation, roles and responsibilities of lead teachers, and process improvements such as textbook selections. Our maintenance department often had conflicting schedules with our curriculum department over such processes as scheduling summer school, end-of-year tests, and leadership training weeks. It was not unusual for maintenance workers to schedule

Instruction	Food service	Finance–accounting	Instructional support	HR	IT

Figure 7.2 Most education organizations are organized functionally.

construction, maintenance, or grass cutting during end-of-year testing or during summer school weeks. The ultimate lack of communication usually centered on the information technology department. Quite often training and events that required technology were scheduled without checking with the IT department to ensure availability of the information and resources. We realized that we were very much a functional process organization.

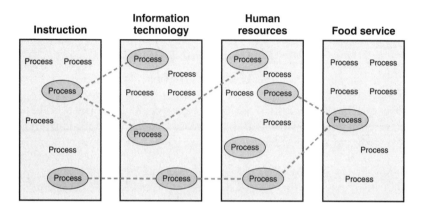

Figure 7.3   Most processes are cross-functional.

Functions

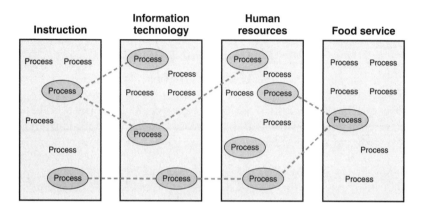

Figure 7.4   Education functional silos don't deal well with cross-functional processes.

The key driver that moved us toward a process-centered organization was not the training, it was the reality of our financial position. Our school system was among the 10 lowest in North Carolina in terms of per-pupil expenditures, and the recession was beginning to impact the businesses in our community. We knew that eventually the tax funding would be impacted. We finally had the sense of urgency to focus on process management and the support, training, and coaching from APQC and ASQ to do the work.

I–SS MODEL FOR PROCESS MANAGEMENT

Over the last 18 months, I–SS has begun to move toward a process-centered organization that focuses on processes rather than functional silos. We started by clearly defining our enterprise (Figure 7.5). What were the

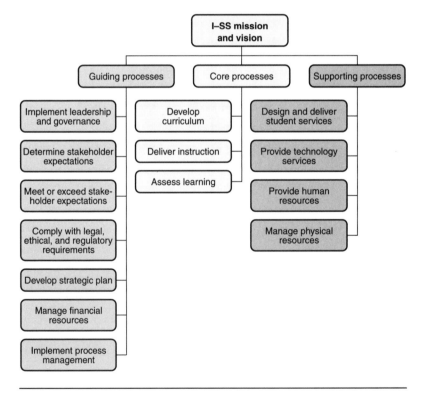

Figure 7.5   I–SS enterprise model.

higher-level core, guiding, and supporting processes? In other words, we took a 30,000-foot level look at our school system and defined our work.

Once we had clearly defined our enterprise, we needed a tool to document the SIPOC (supplier, inputs, process steps, outputs, customers). Also, we received training that helped us understand that we needed to examine the guides such as school board policy, laws, federal and state regulations that directed or guided the process. Additionally, we needed to look closely at enablers such as human resources, information technology, and facilities that support the process. The model we utilized was a model first developed by the military and based on the early work of Juran and Deming. It was called an IGOE, for inputs, guides, outputs, and enablers (Figure 7.6).

We began our work on process management with one of the most crucial of processes in our enterprise—managing financial resources. We had a sense of urgency because the state had requested a midyear return of over $1 million and we were beginning to anticipate the loss of between five percent to 10 percent of funding from state and local sources. Our first step in the process management approach was to define the key subprocesses within the "managing financial resources" overall process and the key departments that work on these subprocesses (Figure 7.7).

We then defined the activities and owners for the key activity of "control financial resources" (Figure 7.8).

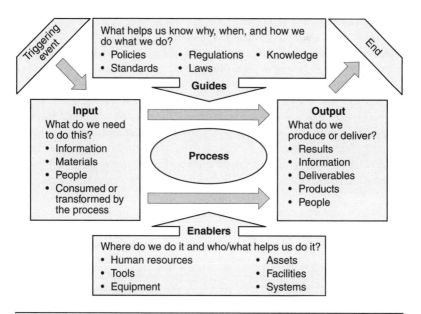

Figure 7.6   The IGOE model.

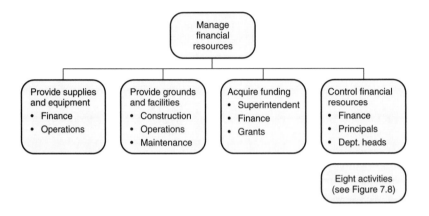

Figure 7.7   Manage financial resources to activity level.

Then we developed an IGOE for the "control financial resources" sub-process (Figure 7.9). A very important step in the IGOE process is to make certain we know the key customers of the outputs from the activities (Figure 7.10) and their expectations or requirements for the outputs.

Our next step was to finalize the IGOE for the control financial resources subprocess and conduct a health check on the degree of satisfaction with the inputs and outputs from the subprocess.

Our health check of the process revealed numerous improvement possibilities. Our HR and finance departments did not reconcile allotments on a regular basis. Our school bookkeepers had large numbers of returned or non-process requisitions and purchase orders. This finding led us to review the steps in the activity of submitting a requisition or purchase order, and we discovered that principals and bookkeepers needed additional training and support with the information technology system and how to read the monthly budget reports. Our finance department had a large number of errors and reworks that have since been eliminated as a result of the training. As a result of our work in this area, we were able to return the $1 million to the state, reduce local spending by over $3 million, and prepare for the eventual eight percent reduction in local funding. Even though I–SS was already one of the lowest-funded districts in per-pupil expenditures in North Carolina, we were able to find even more waste and redundancy in our operations. It is with confidence that we recommend this approach to school systems and predict that school systems nationwide could reduce waste and redundancy of operations by at least 10 percent if they deploy this process with fidelity. The key is starting with a sense of urgency and starting with only one or two key subprocesses all the way to the

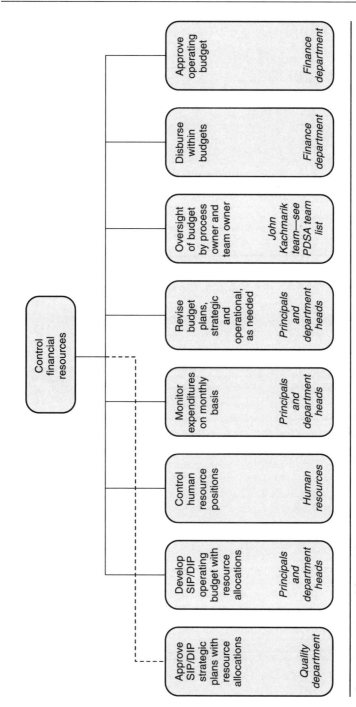

Figure 7.8   Control financial resources to activity level.

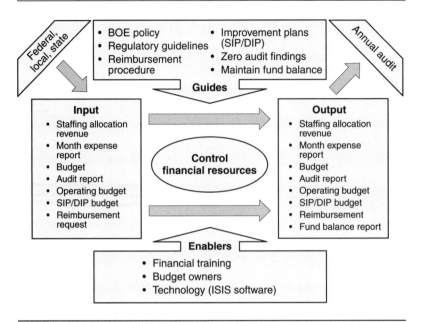

Figure 7.9 IGOE for "control financial resources" subprocess.

External stakeholder	Requirement	Output
Department of public instruction	External audit	Audit report
Taxpayer	Meet legal and ethical requirements Provide education at low cost	Audit report Tax rate
Board of commissioners	Meet legal and ethical requirements Provide education at low cost	Audit report Monthly budget amendments Tax rate
Internal stakeholder	**Requirement**	**Output**
Board of education	Audit findings Fund balance Meet legal and ethical requirements	Audit report
Principals and department heads	Process expenditure requests Approve budgets Approve position requests	Payments Approved budgets Staff allocation matrix
Senior leadership	Monitor expenditures Meet legal and ethical requirements	Monthly expenditure reports Variance reports Position allocation reports Audit reports

Figure 7.10 Stakeholder analysis for "control financial resources" subprocess.

activity level. Trying to do this work for every enterprise process all the way to the activity level would not be possible for any organization to attempt simultaneously.

WHERE ARE WE NOW?

For the 2008–09 school year we implemented a cross-functional model of plan–do–study–act teams at the district level. Each PDSA team had representation from the three major divisions—superintendent, learning, and operations. Our key PDSA teams were: An International Baccalaureate Team, because we wanted to implement an IB choice program to attract charter, private, and homeschool parents. A Behavior Intervention Team, because we wanted to reduce the rate of out-of-school suspension (OSS) for all students and close the gap between white students and African-American students. A Dropout Prevention Team, because we have a district goal of becoming the first large school system to have a 100 percent graduation rate. A Student Wellness Team, because we wanted to reduce childhood obesity and its impact on student wellness and student achievement. A Staff Wellness Team, because we wanted to improve teacher/staff attendance and reduce health care costs. Of course, we also implemented the Control Financial Resources Team already mentioned. The Student Assessment Team was charged with implementing training that would move our teachers to develop and use kid-friendly learning standards and common formative assessments. Finally, the Academic Interventions Team was charged with documenting the academic interventions being used in our system, their related costs, effectiveness of the interventions, and finalizing recommendations for tier 2 interventions of our *response to intervention* model.

The PDSA teams are populated with representation from all relevant departments that may have some alignment with the overall process being developed and deployed. Team members also come from appropriate community, school, parent, and student groups. The teams meet on a regular basis to develop deployment plans and track progress. We ensure accountability through a monthly report-out at our administrative team meeting. The PDSA teams all report out the answers to the following questions:

- Strengths?

- OFIs (opportunities for improvement)?

- Information or data needed?

- Next steps and resources needed?

The monthly reports are then summarized and sent to schools with rec-ommendations as to what next steps schools can take to assist with district process management. For example, the PDSA team on student wellness recommended additional training for all physical education teachers on the use of our Fitness Gram measure and then met with those prin-cipals whose teachers were not deploying the measure with fidelity. The PDSA team for behavioral interventions addressed the need for certain schools whose OSS data were not improving to have additional expecta-tions and training for our *positive behavior support* model. Through this monthly approach, the school board is advised of any changes needed in resource allocation. The PDSA rubric (Figure 7.11) and radar tracking chart

0%	• No systematic approach is evident • The approach is not deployed or very little of it is deployed. • Improvement is achieved by reacting to problems. There is no evidence of an improvement process (PDSA). • There is no alignment between improvements and goals.
20%	• There is beginning development of a systematic approach (a deployment plan).
25%	• The approach is in the early stages of deployment in some areas.
30%	• Early stages of transitioning from reacting to problems to using a PDSA to improve the process.
35%	• The approach is aligned to your goals and to the goals of the district.
40%	• A systematic approach is apparent.
45%	• The approach is deployed, although some areas may be in the early stages of deployment.
50%	• The beginning of a systematic process for evaluation of the approach is evident.
55%	• The approach is in the early stages of alignment with other schools and departments.
60%	• A well-defined systematic approach is evident.
65%	• The approach is well deployed throughout the organization, although, there may be some variation.
70%	• The approach has been through multiple cycles of improvement using a fact-based, systematic process of evaluation.
75%	• The approach is aligned with other schools and departments.
80%	• A well-defined, effective systematic approach is evident.
85%	• The approach is well deployed with little or no variation.
90%	• The approach has been through many cycles of improvement and has yielded sustainable high results through a fact-based, systematic process of evaluation that results in innovation.
100%	• There is evidence that the approach has resulted in organizational sharing and learning.

Figure 7.11   PDSA radar chart reporting rubric.

Third Quarter District PDSA Radar Scores

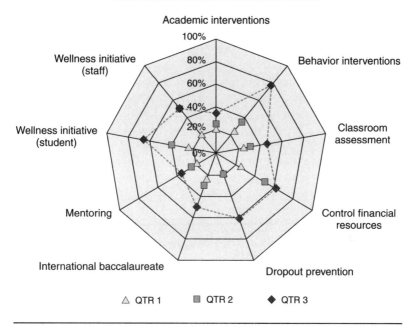

PDSA monthly tracking radar chart.

(Figure 7.12) help ensure that the process of reporting is systematic. The superintendent is made aware of any principal issues that might need to be addressed in evaluation. Every department in the school system understands its role and responsibility in implementing district processes. We continue to struggle with people issues; however, we now have a clear management approach to those key processes that will lead to improvements in not only student learning outcomes but also in operations outcomes. Our continued goal of being a top-ten academic performer in North Carolina while maintaining costs at the bottom-ten level is what Deming would say is *quality* up and *costs* down!!! The process-centered and process management approach to our leadership will not only ensure that we continue our performance but will also set us apart from the school systems with whom we compare, and will eventually result in even higher performance for our school system.

We summarize our work by once again showing the process management approaches that have led to significant improvements in student learning results (Figure 7.13) and operational results (Figure 7.14).

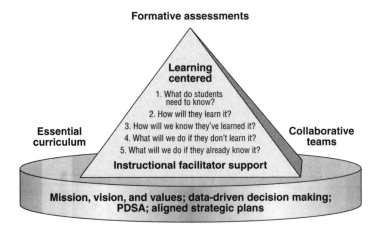

Figure 7.13   I–SS model to raise achievement and close gaps.

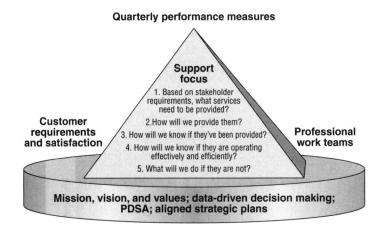

Figure 7.14   I–SS model for aligned, effective, and efficient operations.

From 2002 to 2008, we have seen the following results from this integrated model:

- Academic composite   55th to 9th

- Graduation rate   53rd to 11th (61 percent to 81 percent)

- SAT   57th to 7th (991 to 1056)

- 3–8 Reading   75th to 20th
- 3–8 Math   68th to 12th
- Reading gap AA   Reduced by 48 percent
- Reading gap EC   Reduced by 53 percent
- Computer skills   68 percent to 96 percent (2009)
- Dropout rate   106th to 10th
- Attendance rate   55th to 3rd

OTHER AREAS OF IMPROVEMENT

Bus discipline reduced 50 percent; energy savings of over $4 million; faith-based partners from zero to over 80; highly qualified teachers from 80 percent to 98 percent; overtime costs reduced by 75 percent; child nutrition is a self-sustaining process with over $500,000 provided to the school system for indirect costs; maintenance/custodial workers' compensation ratio among best in North Carolina; fund balance from zero to over $9 million; credit recovery of over 2000 courses, which provide a savings estimated at $2 million for rework. All of this was done with expenditures per pupil in the bottom 10 among North Carolina public schools. I–SS spends $700 less per pupil than the state average.

IN CONCLUSION

We are often asked about the cost of Baldrige. Our response is that quality is not a cost; it is a requirement if school systems and business are to survive in this period of uncertainty and economic upheaval. We are sending our children forward as messengers to a time that we will not see. The question for us is: are we preparing them to deal with the uncertain times that they will surely face? We believe that through the use of the Baldrige Criteria and a commitment to process management and continuous improvement, we will not only prepare our children for the future, we will improve the conditions that they will find in the future. Never before has the sense of urgency for education reform been so important to the survival of our nation and our children's future. Please join us in this important work! Thank you for taking the time to read about our story, and best wishes as you go about the work of changing your classroom, your school, your district, your team, or your organization.

Appendix A
Zero-Based Budgeting Process for Iredell–Statesville Schools

GOALS OF PROCESS

- Ensure funds are spent in most effective and efficient manner possible
- Ensure funds are spent according to customer/stakeholder requirements
- Ensure funds are spent in alignment with strategic plan
- Identify potential reductions and/or redirections of resources
- Educate building- and district-level leadership concerning budget and allocation processes

STEPS IN PROCESS

- Budget owner develops proposed budget by purpose code
- Budget owner identifies key processes in purpose code (core or support)
- Budget owner identifies alignment of purpose code and process with strategic priority (best fit)
- Budget owner identifies customer/stakeholder requirements for each process within the purpose code
- Budget owner identifies current expenditures by function code within purpose code

- Budget owner identifies the strategic indicator that current expenditures are impacting and presents evidence of positive impact on strategic indicator

- Budget owner defends continuation, expansion, or reduction of budgeted amount

BUDGET COMMITTEE

The budget committee comprises the superintendent, CFO, and principal representatives from elementary, middle, and high school levels. The budget committee is charged with presenting a prioritized list of continuation, expansion, and reduction/redirection items to the Budget and Finance Committee of the board of education.

STEPS IN PROCESS FOR BUDGET COMMITTEE

- Review all reports from budget owners

- Identify continuation, expansion, and reduction/redirection items and amounts

- Obtain feedback from all stakeholder groups—teachers, parents, and administrators

- Prioritize expansion and reduction/redirection items based on stakeholder feedback

- Present priorities to Budget and Finance Committee

Appendix B

Roles and Responsibilities of the Instructional Facilitators— Iredell–Statesville Schools, 2008–2009

Focus area	Instructional Facilitator's role	Not the Instructional Facilitator's role
1. District requirements and responsibilities	• Work with the school leadership team to plan for, train, coach, and otherwise facilitate the deployment of the I–SS Model to Raise Achievement and Close Gaps as defined by the I–SS PLC/School Leadership Team Matrix • Attend all Instructional Facilitator (IF) meetings, training events, and other events as directed by the Quality Assurance Division • Attend and participate in regularly scheduled, weekly school leadership team meetings • Address in weekly leadership team meetings discussion of district initiatives and IF responsibilities • Gather and provide feedback on the use of processes in the I–SS Model—Curriculum and Instruction Guides, Predictive Assessments, Professional Learning Communities, or other as directed by the Quality Assurance Division	• Attend meetings or training outside the school unless required or approved by the IF coach • Accept responsibilities in conflict with this document without approval of the IF coaches • Miss a district-required meeting or training event in order to perform a school duty or participate in a school activity without prior approval of IF coach

Continued

Continued

Focus area	Instructional Facilitator's role	Not the Instructional Facilitator's role
	• Schedule time to comply with district requests for data and/or other information, to document work, and to respond to e-mails • Meets all assigned due dates as directed by the Learning Division • Notify the IF coach as far in advance as possible of any absence or obligation that conflicts with district responsibilities • Abide by the roles and responsibilities addressed in this document and as defined by the Instructional Facilitator contract addendum—IF Agreement	
2. School leadership	• Meet weekly with the leadership team to plan for and monitor deployment of the I–SS Model to Raise Achievement and Close Gaps as directed by the I–SS PLC/School Leadership Team Matrix • Coach leadership team and other school leaders in use of quality tools and processes to improve effective and efficient operations	• Act as principal or assistant principal • "Cover" for the principal in an administrative capacity because the principal is out of the building, except in an emergency situation • Be solely responsible to complete paperwork assigned to the principal not aligned to the roles and responsibilities of the IF
3. School improvement team	• Serve, if elected, on SIT and serve as ex-officio member if not elected • Participate with leadership team and SIT chair in planning SIT agendas • Facilitate and/or participate in activities during SIT meetings	• Serve as SIT Chair • Be responsible for SIT meeting agendas

Continued

Continued

Focus area	Instructional Facilitator's role	Not the Instructional Facilitator's role
4. School improvement planning and deployment	• Assist principal/leadership team in organizing and scheduling committees/teams to work on school improvement planning and deployment • With the leadership team, coach the use of systematic process data analysis to identify gap areas, SMART goals, action steps, and deployment plans for the School Improvement Plan (SIP) • Work with leadership team, priority committees/goal teams to ensure staff development is aligned to action steps and deployment plans in SIP • Coach priority committees/goal teams as they work to monitor deployment of the SIP • Facilitate, assist with, or coach, as appropriate, the conducting of district systematic processes for analyzing data, for quarterly monitoring of the SIP, for mid- and end-of-year SWOT, and for school • Attend and assist in the preparation for the first- and third-quarter SIP coaching conferences	• Be directly responsible for monitoring deployment of or compliance for the SIP • Be accountable for SIP checklist • Be responsible for identifying, collecting, and/or organizing data for SIP data analysis • Be responsible for clerical duties associated with school improvement such as making copies for meetings, typing documents, minutes, feedback forms, making revisions, and so on • Attend all goal/priority team meetings • Be assigned as a goal/priority team chair
5. Professional development	• Provide professional development for district initiatives (HYIS, CASL, Differentiation) in addition to CCI elements and PDSA as indicated by the Professional Development Survey, TWCS, and/or the I–SS PLC/School Leadership Team Matrix • Assist in gathering/ordering staff development materials • Use quality tools to gather data on the effectiveness of training and coaching provided by the IF	• Require attendance or develop consequences for failure to attend staff development events • Train True North Logic (TNL) or type names in the Truth North Logic system or otherwise be responsible for TNL system data for the school

Continued

Continued

Focus area	Instructional Facilitator's role	Not the Instructional Facilitator's role
	• Provide training and coaching on Continuous Classroom Improvement (CCI) to Initially Licensed Teachers (Beginning Teachers) as directed by the district (and other as determined by the school) • Coach and monitor deployment of the district's CCI demonstration classroom model with identified volunteers • Coach and assist teachers and/or the leadership team in the completion of TNL templates • Provide written feedback regarding CCI deployment as directed	• Set requirements for implementation of SD • Evaluate implementation as a compliance or personnel issue • Being responsible for the completion/submission of the TNL templates
6. Curriculum and instruction	• Be knowledgable of the NC Standard Course of Study (NCSCOS), how to access it, and related resources on the Web • Help locate resources for teachers • Advocate for teachers for materials needed • Train and coach teacher teams on instructional programs supported by or required by the district or by the SIP, or obtain qualified trainer • Facilitate textbook adoption process as determined by the Curriculum Division	• Develop unit plans for teachers • Observe teachers for purposes of evaluation • Order, purchase, or collect instructional materials • Prepare materials for units of study • Make curriculum or instructional requirements of teachers • Order or count textbooks • Establish requirements for or evaluate teacher compliance with instructional and curriculum expectations of teachers

Continued

Continued

Focus area	Instructional Facilitator's role	Not the Instructional Facilitator's role
7. Planning for instruction	• Coach teams of teachers in developing instructional plans aligned to Curriculum and Instruction Guides and as defined in the I–SS PLC/School Leadership Team Matrix • Coach teacher teams on including quality tools, high-yield instructional strategies, and other best practices in instructional planning in order to plan for, monitor, measure, and improve instruction • Coach teachers to write and implement high-quality lesson plans as needed	• Determine lesson plan requirements • Evaluate or monitor lesson plans • Develop lesson plans for teachers
8. Assessment	• Be knowledgable about the assessment processes and timelines • Collect plus/deltas on Predictive Assessment process and forward data to Curriculum Division • Facilitate and/or coach analysis of assessment results data with teacher teams (and individual teachers as needed) • Coach teacher teams in using data analysis to adjust and improve instruction	• Train teachers on test administration • Serve as testing coordinator for state or district tests
9. Classroom improvement planning and deployment	• Provide training, coaching, and support for the implementation of the I–SS Model to Raise Achievement and Close Gaps as defined by the PLC/School Leadership Team Matrix and this document • Facilitate or otherwise work with professional learning communities to address the I–SS Model and its five key learning-centered questions • Provide training, coaching, and support for the use of Curriculum and Instruction Guides to answer key learning-centered questions 1 and 2	• Evaluate teachers • Observe teachers for evaluation purposes • Participate in any part of the IGP process other than coaching on the NC Teaching Standards • Be solely responsible for the monitoring and completion of the QAR reports

Continued

Continued

Focus area	Instructional Facilitator's role	Not the Instructional Facilitator's role
	• Provide training, coaching, and support for the use of Predictive Assessments to answer key learning-centered question 3 • Provide coaching and support for differentiation to answer key learning-centered questions 4 and 5 • Provide training, coaching, and support to teacher teams in the use of quality tools and processes to monitor classroom learning systems • Provide teacher teams with information from the district in a timely fashion • Train and coach teacher teams on the use of NC Professional Teaching Standards to build high-performing classrooms as directed by the I–SS PLC/School Leadership Team Matrix • Participate in Classroom Walk-Through and use CWT data to determine staff professional development needs and coaching priorities • Assist leadership team in the monitoring of the compliance of the teamwork matrix and completion of the QAR reports	
10. Support services— AIG and GIST, A-Team, EC, ESL	• Be knowledgable of roles and responsibilities of support services committees, and coach committee chairs on the use of Quality Tools and processes as needed • Serve on GIST and A-Team • Coach teacher teams (and individual teachers as needed) on differentiation strategies as they work to meet the learning needs of individual students	• Chair the GIST or A-Team • Serve as LEA on IEP teams except on an emergency basis

Continued

Continued

Focus area	Instructional Facilitator's role	Not the Instructional Facilitator's role
	• Help locate resources for teacher teams and individual teachers • Coach teachers on how to use a continuous improvement approach to help students manage their own learning system and improve performance • Train and coach teacher teams on effective use of Student Support Plans • Coach teacher teams on use of CogAT testing results to plan for meeting students' instructional needs • Attend IEP team meetings as regular ed. representative occasionally (if regular ed. teacher is absent or unavailable, for example)	• Be responsible for evaluating, maintaining, or otherwise monitoring portfolios, files, or other paperwork on AIG or EC students • Create units of study or lesson plans for teachers • Coordinate or oversee administration of CogAT or any other support services required testing
11. Remediation and/or tutoring	• Coach teachers teams on effective use of Student Support Plans • Work with principal and teachers to identify effective remediation or tutoring programs • Work with teacher teams or individuals to identify students who need remediation tutoring services • Work with teachers to identify best practices in addressing differentiated instructional needs of low- and/or high-performing students • Coach the use and deployment of PDSAs that improve effectiveness of remediation and/or tutoring programs • Help locate resources for teachers • Assist leadership team and PLCs in the revision and implementation of the schoolwide intervention continuum	• Oversee scheduling for remediation/tutoring programs • Oversee paperwork for remediation/tutoring programs • Make requirements of teachers concerning remediation/tutoring • Be personally responsible for or involved in regular tutoring or remediation of students

Continued

Continued

Focus area	Instructional Facilitator's role	Not the Instructional Facilitator's role
12. Other duties as assigned	• Attend to bus duty, cafeteria duty, hall duty, ballgame duty, concession stand, or any other duty as assigned to any classroom teacher • Attend PTO meetings and other after-school events as expected of any classroom teacher • *In an emergency situation, comply with any directive given by the principal and/or address any need, even if it conflicts with this document*	• Have extra duties assigned over and above what is expected of any classroom teacher • Be responsible for or oversee discipline, transportation, volunteer programs/hours, yearbook, or other duties or projects that are not encompassed in the role of the Instructional Facilitator and/or that may require the IF's time before, during, or immediately after school when the IF is to be available to teachers

8/03/09

Appendix C
Plan–Do–Study–Act Template Examples

What do we need to learn?

Plan

 Based on the data, our learning target for this week is (SCOS focus):

_____

_____

 We will measure our learning by (when and how):

_____

_____

 Our class performance goal (measure of success):

_____

_____

We will celebrate improvement by:

_____

 We will celebrate reaching our goal by:

_____

This is our plan for the week beginning: _____

How will our class learn it?

Do

Weekly Classroom Action Plan

To help us reach our goal for this learning target, *our teacher will:*

-

-

To help us reach our goal for this learning target, *we will:*

-

-

Our plan for the week beginning: _____

We will reflect on this plan when we receive data on:

_____

How will we know if we've learned it?

Study

Did we reach our goal? _____

Did we improve? _____

Is there anything else we need to think about to help us understand our data?

_____

_____

_____

_____

Today's date: _____

What will we do if we don't learn it?
What will we do if we already know it?

Act

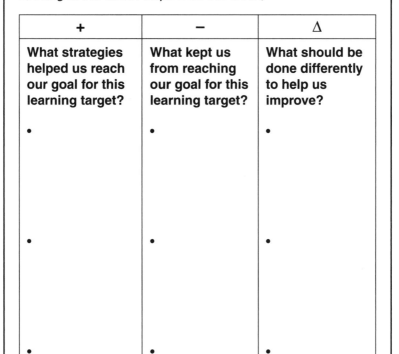

Looking at our action steps from this week,

+	–	Δ
What strategies helped us reach our goal for this learning target?	**What kept us from reaching our goal for this learning target?**	**What should be done differently to help us improve?**
•	•	•
•	•	•
•	•	•

Today's date: _____

What do we need to learn?

Plan

from _____ to _____
             Date   Date

Based on the data, our learning target (objective) for this week is:

_____

_____

_____

We will measure our learning by (when and how):

_____

_____

_____

Our class performance SMART goal:

_____

_____

_____

We will celebrate improvement by:

_____

We will celebrate reaching our goal by:

_____

How will our class learn it?

Do

Classroom Strategies

Our learning strategies for the week beginning:

_____

To help us reach our goal this coming week, *our teacher will:*

•

•

To help us reach our goal this coming week, *we will:*

•

•

We will reflect on this plan when we receive data on:

_____

How will we know if we've learned it?

Study   For the week ending _____

Looking at our data from this week,

Did we reach our goal? _____

Did we improve? _____

What else do the data tell us?   _____

_____

Looking at our action plan from this week,

+	Δ
What strategies helped us learn this week?	**What strategies need to be improved?**
•	•
•	•
•	•
•	•
•	•

What will we do if we don't learn it?
What will we do if we already know it?

Act

Reflection on our classroom action plan (strategies):

Next week our teacher will do the following things differently:

•

•

Next week students will do the following things differently:

•

•

This classroom reflection was completed on: _____
                                                        Date

Name: _____   Teacher: _____

Elementary

Plan   Today's date: _____

My learning target for this week (SCOS focus):

_____

How and when I will measure my learning:

_____

My performance goal:

_____

I will celebrate improvement by:

_____

Do

Strategies I'll use for the week beginning:

_____

To help me reach my goal for this learning target, I will:

•

•

•

Act

+	–	Δ
What strategies helped me reach my goal for this learning target?	What kept me from reaching my goal for this learning target?	What should I do differently to help me improve?
•	•	•
•	•	•
•	•	•

Study

My data chart is on the next page.

For the week ending: _____

Did I reach my goal? _____

Did I improve? _____

What else do my data tell me about my progress?

_____
_____
_____
_____
_____

Bibliography

Barber, Michael, and Mona Mourshad. 2007. *How the World's Best School Systems Come Out on Top.* Chicago: McKinsey and Company.

Barker, Tom. 2006. *Leadership for Results: Removing Barriers to Success for People, Projects, and Processes.* Milwaukee: ASQ Quality Press.

Barth, Roland, Rebecca DuFour, Robert Eaker, and Barbara Eason-Watkins. 2005. *On Common Ground: The Power of Professional Learning Communities.* Bloomington, IN: Solution Tree.

Collins, James C. 2001. *Good to Great.* New York: HarperCollins.

Conyers, John G., and Robert Ewy. 2004. *Charting Your Course: Lessons Learned During the Journey toward Performance Excellence.* Milwaukee: ASQ Quality Press.

Deutschman, Alan. 2007. *Change or Die.* New York: HarperCollins.

DuFour, Richard, Rebecca DuFour, and Robert Eaker. 2008. *Revisiting Professional Learning Communities at Work.* Bloomington, IN: Solution Tree.

Fullan, Michael. 2005. *Leadership & Sustainability: System Thinkers in Action.* Thousand Oaks, CA: Corwin Press.

———. 2006. *Turnaround Leadership.* Jossey-Bass education series. San Francisco: John Wiley & Sons.

———. 2008. *The Six Secrets of Change.* Jossey-Bass education series. San Francisco: John Wiley & Sons.

Hammer, Michael. 1996. *Beyond Reengineering: How the Process-Centered Organization Is Changing Our Work and Our Lives.* New York: HarperCollins.

Jenkins, Lee, L. O. Roettger, and C. Roettger. 2007. *Boot Camp for Leaders in K–12 Education.* Milwaukee: ASQ Quality Press.

Kotter, John P. 1996. *Leading Change.* Boston: Harvard Business School Press.

———. 2008. *A Sense of Urgency.* Boston: Harvard Business School Press.

Marzano, Robert J. 2003. *What Works in Schools.* Alexandria, VA: ASCD.

Marzano, Robert J., and J. Timothy Waters. 2009 *District Leadership That Works: Striking the Right Balance.* Bloomington, IN: Solution Tree.

Reeves, Douglas B. 2008. *Reframing Teacher Leadership.* Alexandria, VA: ASCD.

Scholtes, Peter, David Bayless, Gabriel Massaro, and Nancy Roche. 1994. *The Team Handbook for Educators: How to Use Teams to Improve Quality.* Madison, WI: Joiner Associates.

Index

Belong to the Quality Community!

Established in 1946, ASQ is a global community of quality experts in all fields and industries. ASQ is dedicated to the promotion and advancement of quality tools, principles, and practices in the workplace and in the community.

The Society also serves as an advocate for quality. Its members have informed and advised the U.S. Congress, government agencies, state legislatures, and other groups and individuals worldwide on quality-related topics.

Vision

By making quality a global priority, an organizational imperative, and a personal ethic, ASQ becomes the community of choice for everyone who seeks quality technology, concepts, or tools to improve themselves and their world.

ASQ is...

- More than 90,000 individuals and 700 companies in more than 100 countries
- The world's largest organization dedicated to promoting quality
- A community of professionals striving to bring quality to their work and their lives
- The administrator of the Malcolm Baldrige National Quality Award
- A supporter of quality in all sectors including manufacturing, service, healthcare, government, and education
- YOU

ASQ®

Visit www.asq.org for more information.

ASQ Membership

Research shows that people who join associations experience increased job satisfaction, earn more, and are generally happier*. ASQ membership can help you achieve this while providing the tools you need to be successful in your industry and to distinguish yourself from your competition. So why wouldn't you want to be a part of ASQ?

Networking

Have the opportunity to meet, communicate, and collaborate with your peers within the quality community through conferences and local ASQ section meetings, ASQ forums or divisions, ASQ Communities of Quality discussion boards, and more.

Professional Development

Access a wide variety of professional development tools such as books, training, and certifications at a discounted price. Also, ASQ certifications and the ASQ Career Center help enhance your quality knowledge and take your career to the next level.

Solutions

Find answers to all your quality problems, big and small, with ASQ's Knowledge Center, mentoring program, various e-newsletters, *Quality Progress* magazine, and industry-specific products.

Access to Information

Learn classic and current quality principles and theories in ASQ's Quality Information Center (QIC), *ASQ Weekly* e-newsletter, and product offerings.

Advocacy Programs

ASQ helps create a better community, government, and world through initiatives that include social responsibility, Washington advocacy, and Community Good Works.

Visit www.asq.org/membership for more information on ASQ membership.

*2008, The William E. Smith Institute for Association Research